P R A I S E   F O R

INTERCESSORY PRAYER

Intercessory Prayer has deservedly become a popular classic. This engaging and practical book has contributed enormously to the prayer movement of the last decade. Although thousands of books have been written about prayer, I tend to recommend just four titles wherever I go: *Letters to Malcolm* by C. S. Lewis, *Prayer: Finding the Heart's True Home* by Richard Foster, *The Soul of Prayer* by P. T . Forsythe, and the book you are now holding in your hands. May it impact your life the way it has impacted mine.

Pete Greig
Cofounder, 24-7 Prayer
Author, *God on Mute: Engaging the Silence of Unanswered Prayer*

Every praying Christian and intercessor should read this book! *Intercessory Prayer* will revolutionize your prayer life. It contains a depth of revelation found in no other book about intercession.

Cindy Jacobs
Cofounder, Generals International

I am always amazed at how practical and understandable God's Word is when it is explained by Holy Spirit-anointed teachers. I believe God has inspired the truths shared in this book to release an army of intercessors to strategically and powerfully work together with God at this time. I strongly recommend it to all who want to make a difference for the kingdom of God.

Willard Thiessen
President of Trinity Television and Host of *It's a New Day*

STUDY GUIDE

INTERCESSORY PRAYER

How God Can Use Your Prayers to Move Heaven and Earth

DUTCH SHEETS

Regal

From Gospel Light
Ventura, California, U.S.A.

Published by Regal
From Gospel Light
Ventura, California, U.S.A.
www.regalbooks.com
Printed in the U.S.A.

Library of Congress Cataloging-in-Publication Data
Sheets, Dutch.
  Intercessory prayer study guide / Dutch Sheets.
     p. cm.
  Includes bibliographical references.
  ISBN 978-0-8307-4517-3 (trade paper)
  1. Intercessory prayer. I. Title.
  BV210.3.S547 2007
  248.3'2—dc22
                                                                        2007029539

1 2 3 4 5 6 7 8 9 10 / 10 09 08 07

Rights for publishing this book in other languages are administered by Gospel Light Worldwide, an international not-for-profit ministry. For additional information, please visit www.glww.org, email info@glww.org, or write to Gospel Light Worldwide, 1957 Eastman Avenue, Ventura, CA 93003, U.S.A.

CONTENTS

INTRODUCTION

"Intercessory prayer"—you may have heard this term before, but perhaps you're somewhat unsure of what it means to be an intercessor, even though prayer is an integral part of your life. Dutch Sheets's book *Intercessory Prayer* has shed much light on the Church's understanding of the vitally important and spiritually significant role of prayer in the life of every believer. And now, the *Intercessory Prayer Study Guide*, which can be used for both personal and group study, will allow you to delve deeply into the topic of intercessory prayer and will provide opportunities to put what you learn into practice. (If you are facilitating a group study, the Discussion Leader's Guide located at the end of the study guide will be helpful for you, providing discussion questions and suggestions for facilitating the group.)

If you have already read *Intercessory Prayer*, you will want to take out your copy as a reference as you work through the study guide. If you haven't yet read *Intercessory Prayer*, please pick up a copy at your local Christian bookstore. You will need to read the pages referenced in the study guide at the beginning of each section before answering the questions in the study guide.

You will also want to have a Bible available. You will be immersed in God's Word as you go through the study guide. Some of the Bible passages referred to are already quoted in *Intercessory Prayer*. Some passages you will need to look up for yourself. Dutch Sheets quotes from the *New American Standard Bible* most frequently, though he also refers to several other translations. You should be able to use another translation without a problem, but just realize that he is quoting from the *New American Standard Bible* unless otherwise indicated.

As you begin this study, ask God to give you a teachable heart. As you continue to pray this prayer while working your way through the book, you will find that your prayer life has been ignited and empowered by the very God who created you and who longs to accomplish His will through your prayers. Each time you open this book, ask God to open your eyes to the truths He wants to communicate to you; and then begin to practice them. Remember that God has a great adventure planned for you as you partner with Him to see His wonderful will accomplished on Earth. He has promised to guide and empower you, if you will only set out on this great adventure. Ready? Set? Go!

STUDY GUIDE

CHAPTER ONE

THE QUESTION IS . . .

Prayer—bring up the subject and you're likely to get a wide expanse of opinion about this simple yet pervasive part of our spiritual life. Intercessory prayer—bring up this subject and the panorama extends beyond the horizon! Coming to a conclusive, biblical answer regarding the nature and purpose of prayer is as much a quest to ask the right questions as it is to get the right answers.

Confronted with the Unexpected
(pages 15-16)

Sometimes what we expect to happen in response to prayer is not what we actually experience. Dutch shares a personal story of praying for a comatose woman named Diane. He expected that God would immediately answer his prayers for her healing in a quick and dramatic way; however, it didn't work out that way. Instead, he invested hours every week for a full year, slogging through intimidation, humiliation, questioning and soul-searching.

1. When you pray, what do you expect to happen?

_____

_____

_____

In Dutch's case, it was persistent prayer that resulted in Diane's awakening from that coma and enjoying an incredible—and medically inexplicable—miracle. The result of Dutch's waiting that year, continuing to cry out for God's intervention and healing, was not only restoration for Diane but also new understanding, increased faith and deeper fortitude for Dutch. That period of God-decreed waiting allowed a greater work to be done than an immediate healing would have.

Sometimes it seems that our prayers go unanswered. But this doesn't necessarily mean that something is wrong or that we are not in God's will. As we continue to persevere in prayer, God will continue to work and to align whatever it is we are praying for with His perfect plan. The waiting, in many cases, is just as important as the answer. We must pray with sensitivity to what God is saying, not just according to what we are desiring. We must trust that He is at work no matter what we see or do not see.

8. Can you recall a time when God used a period of waiting for answered prayer to strengthen your faith? What was the result?

_____

_____

_____

So Many Questions
(pages 17-20)

We began this study by saying that asking the right questions is vital to getting the right answers. Dutch poses a series of important questions about prayer. Consider each one included below and jot down a quick response based on your understanding of Scripture.

9. Is God's will for a Christian automatically guaranteed or is it linked to prayer and other factors?

_____

_____

_____

10. Why does it take so long to get an answer to prayer?

11. Why do we have to pray for the lost to be saved if that's God's desire anyway?

12. If Satan is defeated and Christ has all authority, shouldn't we just forget about the devil?

13. What exactly is intercessory prayer?

14. Is everything that happens to me or my family allowed by God?

15. How do we "bear one another's burdens" (Galatians 6:2)?

16. Is there a right time for answered prayer, or does the timing depend on me?

_____

_____

_____

God is never offended by honesty. These questions and others like them do not rock His boat. In fact, He welcomes seeking hearts, and He promises to satisfy them.

Read Luke 11:1-13. We can stand before Jesus just as the disciples did and ask, "Lord, teach us to pray" (v. 1). He is not only an awesome and magnificent King but also a tender and caring Father. He is willing to reveal Himself and His ways to those who sincerely want to know. When we ask, He will give. When we seek, we will find.

17. Write out the following Scriptures:

Matthew 7:7-8

_____

_____

_____

James 1:5

_____

_____

_____

18. After reflecting on the ideas presented in this portion of the study, write out a prayer asking God to draw you into closer communion with Him through prayer. Lay out your concerns and questions before Him and allow His Spirit to begin to open the eyes of your heart to see Him more clearly.

_____

_____

_____

CHAPTER TWO

THE NECESSITY OF PRAYER

Perhaps the most fundamental point to address in our study of intercessory prayer is the need for it. After all, if God is the sovereign Ruler over everything ever created and if He has already decreed His will, then why should we pray? What does it matter? Won't God do what He wants anyway?

I Wonder Why
(pages 21-23)

While there are times when we do what God has said without understanding why, this is not the normative, everyday Christian experience—at least it doesn't have to be. God has given us a written revelation of His will and His ways—the Bible—so that we can, through the help of His Spirit, grow in our understanding of Him and His ways. Though we may see "through a glass, darkly" (1 Corinthians 13:12, *KJV*), we still can see!

1. Write out the following verses:

Jeremiah 33:3

_____

_____

_____

1 Corinthians 2:12

_____

_____

_____

Ephesians 1:17

_____

_____

_____

God wants us to know Him and to understand, as best we can, the *whys* of His ways—including why He asks us to pray.

Is Prayer Really Necessary?
(pages 23-24)

2. Consider these quotes about the necessity of prayer:

You can do more than pray *after* you have prayed, but you cannot do more than pray *until* you have prayed. . . . Prayer is striking the winning blow . . . service is gathering up the results.[1]

God shapes the world through prayer. The more praying there is in the world the better the world will be, the mightier the forces against evil. . . . The prayers of God's saints are the capital stock of heaven by which God carries on His great work upon earth. God conditions the very life and prosperity of His cause on prayer.[2]

In light of these quotes, what is your opinion about the need for people to pray?

_____

_____

_____

There is a biblical balance between God's sovereignty and human effort in seeing His will happen on the earth. God's Word provides us with the right perspective on this essential point. If we believe that our prayers are merely religious discipline, then we will not be likely to persevere when we don't see the answers that we expected. But if we can see in the Word that by God's plan our prayers do effect changes in the destinies of others and in the extension of God's kingdom, then we are more likely to take the privilege seriously and devote ourselves to consistent and persistent prayer.

3. How much time do you devote to prayer on a daily basis?

_____

_____

_____

Why do you spend this time in prayer?

_____

_____

_____

4. Do you believe that God's will can be frustrated—or not accomplished—if people do not pray? Why or why not?

_____

_____

_____

God's Original Plan
(pages 24-28)

In Genesis 1–2, we read that God created everything through His word, His crowning creation being Adam. The name Adam means "man; human being."[3] In fact, the actual Hebrew word is *adam*, and it is also used throughout the Old Testament to refer to humanity in general. This shows us that Adam represents all of us; what God intended for Adam, He intended for the entire human race. So what was God's intention?

5. Read Genesis 1:26-28. What was God's intention for Adam in regard to the animals?

_____

_____

_____

What was God's intention for Adam and Eve as a couple?

_____

_____

_____

6. Read Psalm 8:3-8. With what is man crowned?

_____

_____

_____

Over what is man to rule?

_____

_____

_____

It is safe to say that God's intention for Adam was that he have dominion, or rulership, over the earth and everything in it. The Hebrew word for "rule" in Psalm 8:6 is *mashal*, and it carries the ideas of managing, stewarding or governing.[4] In effect, Adam—as well as his descendants—was intended by God to rule the earth as God's steward, or manager.

7. Read Psalm 115:16. What did God give to man?

_____

_____

_____

8. Read Genesis 2:15. What two responsibilities regarding the earth did God assign to Adam?

_____

_____

_____

Adam's job—and the job of those who would come from him—was to guard, protect and manage the earth and its resources. Adam was to be God's representative, enforcing His authority over creation. This would have been an impossible job had not God created him in His image, in His own likeness.

9. Write out Genesis 1:26-27.

_____

_____

_____

_____

The Hebrew word for "image" in verse 27 is *tselem* and carries the idea of a shadow, phantom or illusion.[5] It means that something is so much like the original that at first glance it may be mistaken for the real thing. Adam was so much like his Creator that he could have been considered His shadow.

This is an astounding revelation: Humanity is meant, by divine design, to represent God. Consider the following New Testament Scripture as well. First Corinthians 11:7 says that man is the "image and glory of God." The word used here for "glory" is the Greek word *doxa*, which means "that which causes something to be recognized for what it really is."[6] According to this verse, human beings are the glory of God, and, as such, God is recognized in them. When the rest of creation looked at Adam, it was supposed to see God—and it did!

10. Read Romans 3:23. What happened when Adam sinned?

_____

_____

_____

11. What does Romans 5:12 say about the long-term effects of Adam's sin?

_____

_____

_____

We must be changed back into God's image "from glory to glory" (2 Corinthians 3:18) for this recognition to be realized again.

12. Sum up your thoughts so far about God's intention that humanity be His representative on Earth.

_____

_____

_____

13. How have you seen your life represent God to others?

_____

_____

_____

14. How does this representation relate to prayer?

_____

_____

_____

15. Why do you think God would choose to work through us to establish His plans on Earth, inextricably weaving His will with our choices?

_____

_____

_____

God Works Through the Prayers of His People
(pages 28-35)

Realizing how much authority God has given to us can be overwhelming because of the responsibility that comes with it. In Adam's case, he relinquished that authority by sinning against God; and Satan—that deceiver and thief—gained a place of power in the earth because of it.

16. Read Luke 4:6-7. What did Satan offer to give to Jesus?

_____

_____

_____

How had it "been handed over" to Satan?

_____

_____

_____

17. Read John 12:31; 14:30; and 16:11. What name did Jesus use to refer to Satan?

_____

_____

_____

18. "So complete and final was God's decision to do things on Earth through human beings that it cost God the Incarnation to regain what Adam gave away. . . . Without question, _humans were forever to be God's link to authority and activity on the earth_" (p. 29). How does this statement bridge the gap between God's sovereignty and human effort in prayer?

_____

_____

_____

19. Describe a time when you believe that God's will was done as a result of your prayers.

_____

_____

_____

20. Describe a time when you felt a need to pray, but you did not pray. What was the result?

_____

_____

_____

21. How do you feel about being God's representative on Earth, the one called to extend His authority here?

_____

_____

_____

So if we, as Adam's descendants, are meant to represent God, does everything depend on us? Let's look at some biblical examples and put this whole idea in sound perspective.

22. Read 1 Kings 18, where we find one of the great stories about the prophet Elijah. In verse 1, what does God tell Elijah to do?

_____

_____

_____

In verse 41, after the showdown between Elijah and the prophets of Baal, what does Elijah tell Ahab to do?

_____

_____

_____

In verse 42, what did Elijah do after he made this statement to Ahab?

_____

_____

_____

23. Read James 5:17-18. What was the result of Elijah's prayers?

_____

_____

_____

It was God's idea to send the rain, but Elijah had to pray—and keep praying—until it came to pass. This incident teaches us that even when God
is initiating something, desiring it to be done, He still needs His people to ask for it. Why? Because God has *chosen* to work through people.

24. Read Daniel 9:1-23. Daniel was a godly Jew who had been taken as
    part of the Babylonian captivity of Israel. According to verse 2, how
    did Daniel know that the captivity (i.e., desolation of Jerusalem)
    was to last 70 years?

    _____

    _____

    _____

    In verse 3, what was Daniel's response to this understanding of
    God's plan?

    _____

    _____

    _____

    In verse 21, who came in response to Daniel's prayer?

    _____

    _____

    _____

    According to verse 23, when did the answer to Daniel's prayer actu-
    ally begin?

    _____

    _____

    _____

Paul E. Billheimer wrote, "Daniel evidently realized that intercession had a part to play in bringing the prophecy to pass. God had
made the prophecy. *When it was time for its fulfillment He did not fulfill
it arbitrarily outside of His program of prayer. He sought for a man upon
whose heart He could lay a burden for intercession. . . . As always, God*

made the decision in heaven. A man was called upon to enforce that decision on earth through intercession and faith."[7] Do you agree or disagree with this statement? Why?

_____

_____

_____

Do you think God's plan would have been accomplished if Daniel had chosen not to pray? Why or why not?

_____

_____

_____

Lest you think that God is somehow dependent on people, the Word is clear that God is completely and perfectly independent of anything outside Himself. He is. Period. And He already has all the resources He needs at His fingertips.

25. Write out Acts 17:24-25.

_____

_____

_____

_____

Though He is sovereign and almighty, He has designed the world in such a way that people's choices and decisions impact the course of history. This isn't to negate His power but, rather, to work within His original intention for humanity: that we represent Him on Earth.

Read Ezekiel 22:30. This verse speaks of God looking for someone to "stand in the gap" for others, someone to pray on behalf of others for His will to be established in their lives. When God's people rise up and accept this call to intercession, then His kingdom can truly come and His will can be truly done on this earth. What an incredible opportunity to partner with the God of all creation, representing Him and carrying His authority on this earth!

Notes

1. S. D. Gordon, quoted in Paul E. Billheimer, *Destined for the Throne* (Fort Washington, PA: Christian Literature Crusade, 1975), p. 51.

2. E. M. Bounds, quoted in Paul E. Billheimer, *Destined for the Throne* (Fort Washington, PA: Christian Literature Crusade, 1975), p. 51.

3. James Strong, *The New Strong's Exhaustive Concordance of the Bible* (Nashville, TN: Thomas Nelson Publishers, 1990), ref. no. 120.

4. R. Laird Harris, Gleason L. Archer, Jr., and Bruce K. Waltke, *Theological Wordbook of the Old Testament* (Chicago: Moody Press, 1980), p. 534.

5. Spiros Zodhiates, *Hebrew-Greek Key Study Bible—New American Standard*, rev. ed. (Chattanooga, TN: AMG Publishers, 1990), p. 1768.

6. Ibid., p. 1826.

7. Paul E. Billheimer, *Destined for the Throne* (Fort Washington, PA: Christian Literature Crusade, 1975), p. 107.

CHAPTER THREE

RE-PRESENTING JESUS

We have been called by God to represent—to *re-present*—Him here on Earth, but what does that have to do with intercession? How can we, as intercessors, re-present God? And in light of this, what does it mean to intercede?

Defining Intercession
(pages 38-39)

Ask fellow believers what intercession is and they're likely to describe it as praying for others. Yet, this isn't really correct. It's important to know what is meant by the term "intercessor" before we can rightly apply it to the concept of intercessory prayer.

1. In your own words, write a definition for "intercession."

　　_____

　　_____

　　_____

The dictionary defines "intercede" as "to go or pass between; to act between parties with a view to reconcile those who differ or contend; to interpose; to mediate or make intercession; mediation."[1] In other words, intercession can be thought of as mediating—representing one party to another for any number of reasons. Though often thought of in a legal context, intercession is not limited to courtrooms. If you think of intercession as mediation, or representation, then you'll see it occurs in many common situations: for example, when a mother bridges the gap between two arguing children or when a secretary gives the boss's instructions to another department. Any work of representation, or mediation, is intercession.

2. If you have been part of a formal mediation, describe your experience. How did the mediator represent one party to another?

_____

_____

_____

3. Can you think of informal, day-to-day situations in which intercession occurs? List them here.

_____

_____

_____

Christ, the Ultimate Intercessor
(pages 39-42)

Adam was supposed to represent God on the earth. Adam was the go-between intended to mediate, or intercede, on behalf of God and His creation. Unfortunately, Adam failed; so Jesus came to re-present God on Earth. He became the Intercessor, going between God and humanity. This act of intercession was not prayer. It was His work of representation whereby He bridged the gap that sin had created, enabling us to have access to the Father again.

4. Write out 1 Timothy 2:5-6.

_____

_____

_____

Between whom is Jesus a mediator?

_____

_____

5. Write out 1 John 2:1.

_____

_____

_____

What phrase in this verse demonstrates Jesus' role as a mediator, or intercessor?

_____

_____

6. Dutch sums up this idea by saying, "[Jesus] is now functioning as our representative, guaranteeing our access to the Father and to our benefits of redemption" (p. 41). In your own words, explain how Jesus intercedes for Christians.

_____

_____

_____

Dutch goes on to explain that this intercessory work is twofold: Jesus goes between God and humanity to reconcile them and also between Satan and humanity to break his hold over them, to separate them.

7. Write out 2 Corinthians 5:18.

_____

_____

How does this verse say that God reconciled the world to Himself?

_____

_____

_____

8. Write out Hebrews 2:14-15.

_____

_____

_____

How does this verse say that Jesus brought freedom to people?

_____

_____

_____

_____

9. How have you experienced this twofold work of intercession in your own life?

_____

_____

_____

_____

Now that we have an accurate understanding of intercession, we can apply it to intercessory prayer. The work of mediation that Jesus did on behalf of all humanity is the reason why we can go to the Father to ask that His will be established in people's lives. Dutch says, "Our *prayers* of intercession are always and only an extension of His *work* of intercession" (p. 42). This is why we are told to ask in Jesus' name. Jesus represented us to the Father and then gave us that ministry as well. Asking in His name is asking God to remember our Mediator, Jesus Christ, and the work He did, and so honor our request.

10. Write out the following Scriptures about praying in Jesus' name:

John 14:13-14

_____

_____

_____

John 16:23-24

_____

_____

_____

11. In your own words, explain why we are told to pray in His name.

_____

_____

_____

We can have full confidence that if we ask for things that are in accordance with His will, in Jesus' name, with Jesus Himself as our Mediator, we will enjoy the power of intercessory pryer.

12. Write out 1 John 5:14-15.

_____

_____

_____

13. In your own words, explain the difference between intercession and intercessory prayer.

_____

_____

_____

14. How does Jesus' work of intercession open the door to effective intercessory prayer?

_____

_____

_____

Distributors for God
(pages 42-44)

Considering intercessory prayer in this light, Dutch makes the statement, "When I say our *prayers* of intercession are an extension of His *work* of intercession, the difference is in distributing versus producing. We don't have to produce anything—reconciliation, deliverance, victory, etc.—but rather we distribute. . . . *Our calling and function is not to replace*

God, but to release Him" (p. 43).[2] Jesus gave us a glimpse of this when He fed the five thouand.

15. Read Matthew 14:15-21. What did the disciples want to do in response to the crowd's need to eat?

_____

_____

_____

What did Jesus tell them to do?

_____

_____

_____

What did the disciples have to feed the crowd?

_____

_____

_____

What did Jesus do with what they had?

_____

_____

_____

What resulted?

_____

_____

_____

How does this passage demonstrate the idea of distributing versus producing?

_____

_____

_____

As God's representatives here on Earth, we have the awesome privilege to extend the kingdom of God here. It's not up to us to come up with the power or authority; we merely stand in the gap as go-betweens to see His power and authority reach the lives of others. Approaching prayer in this light relieves us from any obligation to perform: Our intercession simply distributes what God has produced.

16. Consider each of the following statements:

   • The Producer simply wants to distribute through us.
   • The Intercessor wants to intercede through us.
   • The Mediator wants to mediate through us.
   • The Representative wants to represent through us.
   • The Go-Between wants to go between through us.
   • The Victor wants His victory enforced through us.
   • The Minister of Reconciliation has given us the ministry of reconciliation.

   Describe how God has used you in one or all of these ways.

   _____

   _____

   _____

   _____

   How does thinking of intercessory prayer in this way give you more confidence?

   _____

   _____

   _____

   _____

To sum up, intercessory prayer is really a continuation of the work of Jesus through His Body, the Church, to stand in the gap between God and people to see them reconciled to God or between Satan and people to enforce the victory of the Cross in their lives.

17. Write out John 20:21.

_____

_____

_____

What is the chain of authority inferred by this verse?

_____

_____

_____

18. Read 2 Corinthians 5:18-19. How is intercessory prayer a way in which we participate in the ministry of reconciliation?

_____

_____

_____

When we are sent by others, we go in their authority to accomplish whatever work they send us to do. In this way, we are representing them. Through intercessory prayer, we are following God's intention for us to be representatives of Him on the earth. We have the ability to do this only because of Jesus' work on the cross—His perfect and complete intercession.

Why is it important to recognize that we have been sent by God? Because it means that the authority and power are coming from Him, not from us.

19. Reread John 14:12-14. According to this verse, if we have faith in Jesus, what will happen in our lives?

_____

_____

_____

Why must we ask in Jesus' name?

_____

_____

_____

According to verse 14, what can we ask for?

_____

_____

_____

_____

20. Dutch tells of a personal experience along these lines, in which he saw God move through him to bring deliverance and healing. Can you think of a time when God used you as His representative to do a special work on behalf of someone else? What happened?

_____

_____

_____

_____

Dutch makes the point that our prayers of intercession release Christ's finished work of intercession. In His mercy, God has chosen to partner with us to accomplish His will on Earth—it is His sovereign plan. Knowing this, we must ask ourselves, *Will we rise up and accept the challenge to wholeheartedly believe in the victory of Jesus and, as ambassadors of Him, extend that freedom to those around us?* God wants us to trust Him and to effectively re-present Him to the world. He is with us—in us—to see this hapen.

21. In what way do believers re-present Jesus to the world?

_____

_____

_____

22. How has God used you to re-present Himself to someone?

_____

_____

_____

23. Pray that God will open your eyes to see how you can re-present Jesus to those around you. Then write out the names of two people for whom you will begin to consistently pray.

As you pray, be open to God's plan to minister to them. You have been sent by God!

Notes

1. *The Consolidated Webster Encyclopedic Dictionary* (Chicago: Consolidated Book Publishers, 1954), p. 384.
2. R. Arthur Matthews, *Born for Battle* (Robesonia, PA: OMF Books, 1978), p. 106.

CHAPTER FOUR

MEETINGS: THE GOOD, THE BAD AND THE UGLY

Chances are if you're reading this book, you're interested in prayer. And if you're interested in prayer, you've probably attended a prayer meeting or two—or a zillion! Prayer meetings can range from perfunctory and run-of-the-mill to wild and life changing. Though this chapter isn't about church prayer meetings per se, it will explore a particularly important idea about *prayer* and *meeting*.

Boy Meets Girl
(pages 49-52)

Dutch describes three seemingly unrelated events, or meetings: the day he *met* his wife, the day his front teeth *met* with a zooming baseball, and the day that death *met* life through the victory at the Cross. Why such an odd assortment of examples? To illustrate that there are many types of meetings. Just think about how many times you met with someone—or something!—over the past week alone:

- Meetings with bosses
- Meetings with coworkers
- Meetings with friends
- Meetings with teachers
- Meetings with family members
- Meetings with pastors
- Meetings with doctors, accountants, contractors

- Good meetings
- Bad meetings
- Meetings

1. List two important meetings in your life. What happened? Why are they so memorable?

_____

_____

_____

2. The Bible also describes some meetings. Look up the following Scriptures and write down what two things are meeting in each passage:

Psalm 85:10

_____

_____

_____

Amos 4:12

_____

_____

_____

1 Thessalonians 4:17

_____

_____

_____

Any intersection of our lives with someone or something else is a meeting. Sometimes meetings are wonderful; sometimes meetings are difficult. However, the most important meeting occurs through prayer.

The Hebrew word for "intercession" is *paga*, and it means "to meet."[1] Though we often automatically associate intercession with prayer, the true meaning of "intercession" embodies a much broader perspective.

Paga can happen during prayer, but it is not strictly a prayer word. It has many shades of meaning, which we will explore throughout the course of this study. Let's begin with the idea that prayers of intercession create intersections where people can meet with the power of God.

Intercession Creates a Meeting
(pages 52-54)

3. "Intercessors *meet* with God; they also *meet* the powers of darkness" (p. 52). What two meetings are described in this statement?

What do you think this statement means?

Describe a specific instance when you met with God on another's behalf. What happened?

Describe a specific instance when you met the powers of darkness on another's behalf. What happened?

How have other people's prayers impacted your life by bringing you closer to God or by releasing you from the powers of darkness?

_____

_____

_____

Whom do you know who needs an arranged meeting with God
today?

_____

_____

_____

_____

Whom do you know who needs to be released from a meeting with
the powers of darkness?

_____

_____

_____

_____

Simply put, when we pray to God, we are meeting with Him. In prayers
of intercession, we are meeting with Him to ask that He meet with
someone else. We are the go-between, if you will, standing as a representative and asking for God's intervention on someone's behalf. On the
other end of the spectrum, when we stand in a place of spiritual warfare, we are meeting with the enemy to enforce the work of Jesus by
breaking the enemy's hold over someone. How is this possible? Because
of the meeting Jesus had the day He went to the cross. When He offered
His perfect life as a substitute for our sinful ones, the justice of God
met the mercy of God, and we were forgiven; the power of life met the
power of death, and Satan's hold over humanity was defeated.

4. Explain how the Cross was a meeting place for the work of Christ's
   intercession.

_____

_____

_____

5. How does His work of intercession open the door to our prayers of intercession?

_____

_____

_____

6. Write out 2 Corinthians 5:18-19. (This should be a familiar passage to you now!)

_____

_____

_____

On the cross, Jesus re-presented us; now as His representatives, we stand before God, releasing the fruit of that act of intercession and asking that God meet with others. This is *paga*!

As God's representative, take a minute and pray for the two people you listed previously, both the one who needs to meet with God today and the one who needs to be released from a meeting with the powers of darkness.

Meetings That Heal
(pages 54-57)

Dutch gives two examples of the power of this kind of meeting, both of which occurred during a missions trip to Guatemala. In the first situation, Dutch felt impressed to pray for a woman whose ankle had been severely broken. Because of her age, it had not healed well. As Dutch rose to cross the room—stepping between the woman and God to ask for a meeting of His healing with her frailty—the presence of God filled the room. Dutch could not even make it all the way across the room, but stopped halfway, weeping in the powerful presence of the Lord. *Paga*. A meeting happened! The woman's ankle was healed, and she was filled with the Holy Spirit.

Not long after this, Dutch was at a hospital praying for a woman with tuberculosis. As he prayed, the woman next to her, who had been permanently injured when her spinal cord was accidentally cut during an operation, asked to be prayed for. Again, Dutch stood as the go-between, asking God on the woman's behalf that His healing power would meet with her injury. *Paga*. Another meeting created by a prayer of intercession. The woman was not noticeably changed—at first. As Dutch left and made his way to someone else, the woman began to shout, "*¡Milagro!*" (Miracle!), because her body was being restored to wholeness. By the time Dutch returned to the woman's bedside, her injury had been completely healed.

7. Explain how prayer created a meeting in each of these circumstances.

_____

_____

_____

8. Describe a time when you witnessed a miracle.

_____

_____

_____

What part did prayer play in causing that miracle to happen?

_____

_____

_____

In what ways was there a *meeting*?

_____

_____

_____

In both of these healings in Guatemala, a meeting took place, which was possible because of Christ's work as the ultimate Intercessor. What Christ did on the cross makes it possible for God's purposes to be again fulfilled here on Earth. The miracles happened because one of His representatives—in this case, Dutch—stepped out in faith and arranged the meeting. God wants to meet with people. As Dutch points out, "Prayer *meetings* create God *meetings*."

This isn't to infer that miracles of this magnitude will happen every time you pray. But regardless of the perceived outcome, this fact remains: We can bring people into contact with God through prayers of intercession. Sometimes it means a minute of prayer; other times it means days, weeks or years. But however long it takes, it's worth the effort.

9. List a long-standing prayer that you have been bringing before God.

_____

_____

_____

_____

How long have you been praying for this?

_____

_____

What kind of meeting are you praying for?

_____

_____

10. Look up 2 Corinthians 1:11. How was Paul being helped? Why was favor granted to him?

_____

_____

_____

11. Look up Philippians 1:19. Through what two things did Paul expect deliverance to come?

_____

_____

_____

The bottom line is this: As you pray, you are opening the door for a meeting. Though it takes time, do not grow weary and give up. God is faithful, and you will see Him answer your prayers.

She-Bear Meetings
(pages 57-59)

We have looked at the first type of meeting: uniting people with God's presence. Now let's consider meetings that disunite people from the powers of darkness. The word *paga* also has a violent connotation. It is used as a battle term to indicate a confrontation in which someone is defeated.

12. Write out Proverbs 17:12.

_____

_____

_____

What kind of meeting (*paga*) is described in this verse?

_____

_____

_____

What happens when someone gets between a mama bear and her cubs? The bear, in all her strength, rushes to defend her offspring. That is a meeting you avoid at all costs!

When Satan came between God and His people, it was not unlike the fury of that mama bear, and it led to a violent meeting between God and the devil. As our representative, Jesus met Satan on Calvary, and the earth rocked under the force of the battle.

13. Read Matthew 27–28, which record Jesus' crucifixion and resurrection. Describe the physical events that happened on the earth according to the following verses: Matthew 27:45,51-52; 28:2.

_____

_____

_____

14. Look up the following verses and describe what unseen events also occurred during this *paga*:

    Isaiah 61:1; 1 Peter 3:18-19; 4:6

    _____

    _____

    _____

    _____

    Genesis 3:15; Isaiah 53:5; 1 Peter 2:24

    _____

    _____

    _____

    Matthew 28:18

    _____

    _____

    _____

15. Sum up the results, both physical and spiritual, that happened at the meeting of the Cross.

    _____

    _____

    _____

    _____

16. Write out Jesus' words that were recorded in John 19:30.

    _____

    _____

    _____

    What do you think He meant by this?

    _____

    _____

    _____

The Greek word for the phrase "It is finished" is *tetelestai*. When Jesus said this, He was not referring to His death. He was declaring that He had accomplished, or finished, the work that He had come to Earth to do: He had met with God to reunite Himself with His Bride, and He had met with Satan to disunite him from humanity. *Tetelestai* means "paid in full,"[2] and this what Jesus meant when He said it. The debt humanity owed God was paid in full through His death and resurrection.

17. Write out 1 John 3:8.

_____

_____

_____

_____

The Greek word for "destroy" in this verse is *luo*. *Luo* has both a legal and a physical meaning. Legally, it means to pronounce that someone or something is no longer bound or to dissolve or void a contract that is legally binding. Physically, *luo* means to dissolve or melt, break, beat something to pieces, or untie something that is bound.[3] Paul's boat was *broken* by the rocks (see Acts 27:41). One day the earth will *melt* from great heat (see 2 Peter 3:10,12).

18. How does each of these definitions relate to the work of Jesus as our Intercessor?

_____

_____

_____

_____

19. How does knowing what happened at the Cross give you new confidence in prayer?

_____

_____

_____

_____

20. What does Jesus' statement "It is finished" mean to you now?

_____

_____

_____

Enforcing the Victory
(pages 59-62)

This again leads us to our work as His representatives. Spiritual warfare is enforcing the victory that Jesus won on the cross for all humanity. We meet with the powers of darkness in His strength, as His ambassadors, to declare the truth He already secured. The power of Satan has been broken, and we can stand as a go-between to see that victory put into effect.

21. Write out Matthew 16:19 and underline the word "loose."

_____

_____

_____

This is the word _luo_, and Jesus used it to describe what the Church is called to do through spiritual warfare. As His representatives, we meet the powers of darkness to enforce the victory that His work of intercession accomplished.

22. Did Jesus "destroy the works of the devil" (1 John 3:8), or do we? Explain your answer and give an example from your own personal experience.

_____

_____

_____

Summing up this lesson, we as intercessors can meet with God to see others reconciled to Him and to His purpose for their lives, and we can meet with the powers of darkness on behalf of others to enforce the victory accomplished through Jesus' work of intercession on the cross.

Either way, our prayers can create a meeting, and that meeting can bring about a life-changing experience for someone.

23. How does this idea change your idea of a prayer meeting?

_____

_____

_____

Notes

1. Francis Brown, S. R. Driver, and Charles A. Briggs, *The New Brown-Driver, Briggs-Gesenius Hebrew and English Lexicon* (Peabody, MA: Hendrickson Publishers, 1979), p. 803.
2. Spiros Zodhiates, *The Complete Word Study Dictionary* (Iowa Falls, IA: Word Bible Pubishers, 1992), p. 1375.
3. Spiros Zodhiates, *Hebrew-Greek Key Study Bible—New American Standard*, rev. ed. (Chattanooga, TN: AMG Publishers, 1990), p. 1583.

CHAPTER FIVE

CHEEK TO CHEEK

Have you ever watched a couple glide across a dance floor, gracefully steadying each other—hands held tightly and arms linked with confidence—as they sweep from one end of the room to another? They lean cheek to cheek on each other, relying on the strength each of them contributes to the whole, and glide together in perfect time to the music. It's a beautiful sight to watch—even if you yourself have two left feet.

As Christians, we also are part of a dance, one that will echo through the halls of heaven for eternity. And God calls us to the floor to learn to move together, to learn to lean upon each other with the same type of confidence and grace. One way we embrace this kind of unity is through intercessory prayer. How? Read on!

Lean on Me
(pages 63-64)

The Bible makes it clear that we are to stand alongside each other, lending our help and encouragement when needed. Everyone needs some help from time to time. If you think back over your own life, there are probably a few people that especially stand out in your mind as ones who have come alongside you during a difficult time to help bear your burden so that you could make it through. It is this concept of bearing—not unlike dancing cheek to cheek—that we want to focus on now in light of intercessory prayer.

1. Write out the following verses:

   Romans 12:15

   _____

   _____

   _____

   Galatians 6:2

   _____

   _____

   _____

2. Describe a time in your life when someone came alongside you and helped you during a particularly difficult circumstance.

   _____

   _____

   _____

   What specific things did this person do that helped you?

   _____

   _____

   _____

3. How have you been able to help bear another's burden?

   _____

   _____

   _____

   What was the result?

   _____

   _____

   _____

There are two words used in the New Testament that are translated "bear." One of them is _anechomai_ and means "to sustain, bear or hold up against a thing."[1] In other words, it means standing alongside someone in need, letting him or her lean on you for strength.

4. Write out the following verses and underline the word "bear" in each. These are examples of *anechomai*.

Ephesians 4:2

_____

_____

_____

Colossians 3:13

_____

_____

_____

This idea of bearing is like tying a weak plant to a stake: The strength of the stake is transferred to the plant and bears it up.

5. In what ways should the Body of Christ bear each other up?

_____

_____

_____

How have you experienced this?

_____

_____

_____

Carry the Burden Away
(pages 64-69)

The second word translated "bear" is *bastazo*; it conveys the idea of bearing, or carrying, something away—not just lifting or sustaining but removing it.[2] This word is used in Galatians 6:2, when we are told to bear each other's burdens, and in Romans 15:1-3. Read both of those passages now; we will look more in depth at them shortly.

We've looked at how people—including ourselves—are called to bear one another's burdens, but what about Jesus? How did He lift the burden that we carried and take it away? Understanding this allows us to better continue this act of intercession.

Jesus demonstrated both aspects of bearing when He did His work of intercession on our behalf on the cross. Remember that His intercession was not a prayer but a work that reconciled us to God and broke the power of darkness over our lives. When did this work reach its fulfillment? On the Cross!

6. Write out Isaiah 53:6,12 from the *New International Version* or the *King James Version* of the Bible. Underline the words "laid," "bore [bear]" and "intercession."

_____

_____

_____

This whole chapter is a graphic description of Christ's work of intercession. Interestingly, both the words "laid" and "intercession" are translations of the Hebrew word *paga*. Sound familiar? Jesus met with sin on our behalf in the ultimate work of intercession that would free us from sin. Then He "bore" those sins away. The Hebrew word used for "bore" is *nasa* and means to "remove to a distance"[3] or "to bear away."[4] The Greek counterpart to this word is *bastazo*.

7. Write out a quick definition for the following words:

Paga (Hebrew)

_____

_____

Anechomai (Greek)

_____

_____

Bastazo (Greek)

_____

_____

Nasa (Hebrew)

_____

_____

Understanding that this bearing is not a continual carrying, but rather a removing, is essential to our understanding of our part in Christ's intercession. A clear Old Testament type of this bearing is the Day of Atonement. Each year on this day, two goats were brought before the priest. One was sacrificed; the other was used as a scapegoat.

8. Read Leviticus 16:7-10,20-22. Sum up in your own words what happened to each goat.

_____

_____

_____

When the priest placed his hands on the head of the goat and confessed the sins of the people of Israel, the blame was, in effect, being laid on the goat—thus the term "scapegoat." The animal was then sent out into the wilderness, never to be seen again. This was a foreshadowing of Christ's bearing our sins and taking them far away from us.

9. Describe how this is a picture of Jesus' bearing our sins.

_____

_____

_____

10. Write out Psalm 103:12.

_____

_____

_____

What did Jesus do with our sins?

_____

_____

_____

Read the following Scriptures, which expound upon this idea: Romans 6:6 and 1 Peter 2:24.

11. How did Jesus demonstrate both aspects of bearing when He went to the cross on our behalf?

_____

_____

_____

12. Applying this idea to our role as intercessors, Dutch says, "We stake (*anechomai*) ourselves to the person and *carry the burden away* (*bastazo*), helping them *get rid of it!*" (p. 66). Explain how we can, as followers of Jesus, bear one another's burdens in both ways.

_____

_____

_____

13. Write out Colossians 1:24.

_____

_____

_____

In your understanding, what could possibly be lacking in Christ's afflictions?

Our Part
(pages 69-74)

What could possibly be lacking in Christ's afflictions? Our part. This is not to say that we are bearing away sin; Jesus did that once and for all (see Hebrews 10:12). Rather, we share in that work, re-presenting Him through prayers of intercession.

Reread the following passages about bearing one another's burdens: Romans 15:1-3, Galatians 6:2, Ephesians 4:2 and Colossians 3:13. In Ephesians 4:2 and Colossians 3:13, we are called to lift the burdens of others, like the stake alongside a weak plant does. In Romans 15:1 and Galatians 6:2, we are called to carry those burdens away. These four passages cover both aspects of the word "bear." As we re-present Jesus, being the go-between and either seeking reconciliation or enforcing Christ's victory over the powers of darkness, we are implementing the ministry of intercession.

14. "We're not simply to carry burdens *for* others, we're to carry them *away from* others—just as Jesus did. . . . We're not literally *re-doing* what Christ did, we're *re-presenting* what He did" (p. 70). Do you agree with this statement? Why or why not?

_____

_____

_____

15. How have you experienced both aspects of bearing burdens: carrying burdens for others and carrying burdens away from others?

_____

_____

_____

Read the verses below and consider the examples Dutch gives to illustrate how we do our part:

• Jesus is the balm of Gilead (see Jeremiah 8:22), but we apply this healing salve (see James 5:14-16).

• Jesus is the fountain of life (see Jeremiah 2:13; 17:13), but we are dispensers of His living water (see John 4:14).

- Jesus is the comforting shepherd's staff (see Psalm 23:4), but He allows us the privilege of extending it (see 2 Corinthians 1:4).

- Jesus inaugurated the New Covenant with His blood (see Hebrews 12:24), but He has made us ministers of this New Covenant, extending its power to others (see 2 Corinthians 3:6)

16. In your own words, what is the difference between re-doing and re-presenting?

_____

_____

_____

Why is this an important distinction?

_____

_____

_____

How does this relate to our call to intercessory prayer?

_____

_____

_____

Dutch tells the story of a missionary couple in Jamaica whose son was deathly ill with a fever. Though they were strong Christian believers and capable intercessors in their own right, they needed the support of other members of the Body in order for the spirit of infirmity's hold over their son to be broken.

17. When have you experienced a turnaround in a situation for which you asked others to pray with you?

_____

_____

_____

18. Why do you think that we sometimes need the prayer support of others in order to see a circumstance change?

_____

_____

_____

How do the ideas of bearing burdens and fulfilling what is lacking in Christ's afflictions relate to needing prayer support to see a circumstance change?

_____

_____

_____

19. The following quote from the father of the sick boy sums up this point: "Sometimes the covenant of the Lord is released to you through others coming to your aid" (p. 71). Do you agree with this statement? Why or why not?

_____

_____

_____

Enforcing and Treading upon the Enemy
(pages 74-78)

Let's look at some biblical examples of the call we have to re-present Jesus' work of intercession through our prayers of intercession, focusing on the ideas explained in this chapter.

20. Read Joshua 9–10. How did the Gibeonites deceive the Israelites?

_____

_____

_____

Why did they want to deceive them (i.e., what did they want)?

_____

_____

_____

What resulted from their deception?

_____

_____

_____

How does this story demonstrate the power of covenant?

_____

_____

_____

21. Reread Joshua 10:22-24. A very significant event that is often overlooked occurs in this short passage. It evidences so clearly the idea of our call as intercessors to enforce the victory Jesus brought about on the cross. Who were brought to Joshua?

_____

_____

_____

What did he instruct his army commanders to do?

_____

_____

_____

According to custom, the leader of the victorious army would put his feet on the necks of the defeated kings as a sign to all of their obligatory submission. Instead of doing this himself, Joshua had his followers place their feet on those conquered enemies. Joshua is an Old Testament type of Jesus. These three verses point to what Jesus later did for us: He defeated the enemy and then instructed us to enforce the victory.

The enemies of God were crushed *legally* on the cross of Jesus Christ and placed under His feet, and they are crushed *literally* as we do our part and enforce that victory. Through intercessory prayer we place our feet on the defeated enemy's neck and declare that Jesus is Lord!

Read the following verses and note the call upon the Church to extend the victory of the Cross: Luke 10:19, Romans 16:20 and Ephesians 2:6; 3:10.

Read Psalm 110:1-3. This is the messianic prophecy about Christ's rule over His enemies and the extension of that rule through a willing army. Dutch explains, "Christ is looking for a volunteer army that will stretch forth His strong scepter of authority, ruling in the midst of their enemies, enforcing His great victory" (p. 76). Sometimes this requires spiritual warfare on our part. Though the enemy is defeated, he does not easily give up his ground.

22. Why, if Satan is defeated, is there still a need for spiritual warfare?

23. What is your experience with spiritual warfare as it relates to intercessory prayer?

24. Write out Joshua 1:3 and underline the word "treads."

The word "tread" is the Hebrew word *darak*; it connotes violent or war-oriented treading upon something. *Darak* began to be used to mean "bending the bow," such as when an archer readies to shoot an arrow.[5] In Joshua 1:3, God wasn't saying that every place the feet of His people

1. What do you suppose is the link between intercession and boundaries?

   _____

   _____

   _____

It seems a natural connection that *paga* can mean not only "interces-sion" but also "boundary." This is because prayer is an avenue God uses to establish His protective boundaries in our lives.

2. "We CAN build boundaries of protection around ourselves and oth-ers through intercession" (p. 81). Do you agree with this statement? Why or why not?

   _____

   _____

   _____

Launching out into this subject of divine protection, the first concern we face is a seeming conflict between God's sovereignty and the evil that happens all too often. In other words, if God is in control, then whatever happens must be because He has allowed it, right? If so, it really doesn't matter what we do or don't do; whether or not we are pro-tected is based solely upon God. Ultimately, this leads to the question of the necessity of prayer.

3. What do you think: If God is sovereign, if He is controlling every-thing that happens, then why pray?

   _____

   _____

   _____

4. Read the Lord's Prayer from Matthew 6:9-13. Why are we told to pray for God's will to be done if He is sovereignly in control of everything?

   _____

   _____

   _____

5. Read 1 Timothy 2:3-4. According to this passage, what does God want? Does this happen? If it is God's desire, then why isn't it happening?

---

6. Read Hebrews 2:8. What seeming contradiction is presented in this verse?

If all things are under Him (i.e., He has authority over everything), why does this verse say that we don't see all things under Him yet?

Because of our limited perspective, this seems like double-talk; but it really isn't. God has brought an end to the reign of evil. It's a done deal. Now the Church, His Body, has the authority to bring that spiritual victory into a present reality through the grace and power of God.

Governing Principles
(pages 81-85)

The Bible is clear that though the love of God is unconditional, His blessing and favor—or in the case of this study, His protection—are not. They are given to those who meet His conditions. Now before you think this means we have to work for God's blessings, stop. It means nothing of the sort. The following passages provide a glimpse into the biblical resolution to this apparent paradox. Read each verse and then answer the corresponding questions. You will gain confidence in God's provision and a solid understanding of your part in seeing it worked out in your life and in the lives of those you pray for.

7. Read Matthew 17:20; 21:21-22; Mark 11:22-24; and James 1:6-8. What must we have in order to see mountains moved or to receive what we ask for in prayer?

_____

_____

_____

_____

What must we *not* have?

_____

_____

_____

8. Read Mark 11:25-26. Why do you think Jesus talks about forgiveness in the context of answered prayer?

_____

_____

_____

What must we do to experience God's forgiveness in our lives?

_____

_____

_____

9. Read Hebrews 6:12. What two things are needed in order to inherit the promises of God?

_____

_____

_____

10. Read Isaiah 1:19-20. What two things must happen in order to "eat the best of the land"?

_____

_____

_____

11. Read Malachi 3:8-12. Why were the Israelites under a curse?

_____

_____

_____

12. Read Deuteronomy 6:7-8 and Proverbs 22:6. What must we do in order to see our children walk in the ways of the Lord?

_____

_____

_____

13. Read John 15:7. What must we do in order to be given what we ask for in prayer?

_____

_____

_____

14. Read Psalm 91:1. What must we do to "abide in the shadow of the Almighty"? (More on this later!)

_____

_____

_____

15. Read Ephesians 6:11,16. What must we wear in order to stand against the devil and his schemes?

_____

_____

_____

What must we take up in order to extinguish the fiery arrows of the enemy?

_____

_____

_____

16. Read James 4:7 and 1 Peter 5:8-9. What must we do to fend off the devil?

_____

_____

_____

_____

There are many more such passages, but these will lay a strong foundation. To clarify, we do not earn God's acceptance or forgiveness, but once we have been made a part of His family *through His grace*, we must walk in obedience to His Word in order to reap the benefits He longs to bestow. We have a part to play in seeing His blessing in our lives. Why is it this way? Only God knows. He, in His infinite wisdom, set it up this way. We are called—rather, invited—to be a part of the extension of His authority on this earth. And we position ourselves to do so through submitting to what He has required of us in His Word. The key is obedience.

This is not to say that when bad things happen, people have done something wrong or have in some way failed. Many times it is our weakness and sin that open the door to an enemy invader, but not always. Sometimes there is no apparent reason. Yet the message of the Bible remains the same. We are still called by God to obediently and consistently re-present Him and enforce His victory, trusting Him with the outcom.

17. Write out Philippians 2:13.

_____

_____

_____

Who is working in us and for what purpose?

_____

_____

_____

_____

18. How would you now explain the balance between God's sovereignty and our responsibility as it relates to His blessing of protection over our lives?

_____

_____

_____

How does this understanding affect your idea of intercessory prayer?

_____

_____

_____

Dwelling in the Secret Place
(pages 85-86)

Right alongside obedience is consistency. If we want to see spiritual boundaries enforced, we must be consistent in our prayer life.

19. Write out Psalm 91:1. Underline the words "dwells" and "abide."

_____

_____

_____

In this verse, the word "dwell" means "to remain or abide; to dwell in or inhabit."[2] The word for "abide" means, among other things, "to spend the night."[3] Take these definitions and reread the verse, substituting them for the underlined words. Then read the rest of the psalm. The point is well made: We must make our time with God not just an activity but also a lifestyle. This is the only way to build boundaries of protection.

20. Why is consistency a vital part of intercessory prayer?

_____

_____

_____

Being sensitive to the Lord, this mother had had a *kairos* prayer to counter a *kairos* attack.

25. Dutch says, "Although we are promised protection from our enemy, we have a definite part to play in the securing of it for ourselves and for others" (p. 95). Do you agree? Why or why not?

_____

_____

_____

26. Describe a time when you felt a pressing burden to pray for someone right then and there. What happened as a result?

_____

_____

_____

27. If a believer is burdened to pray but does not, do you think that God's will can be waylaid or even thwarted? Why or why not?

_____

_____

_____

God does not want us to feel guilty about failing to pray, so don't allow yourself to be weighed down by condemnation (see Romans 8:1). Instead, take a moment to search your heart and come to a renewed commitment to be sensitive to pray. Then lay your heart before the Lord and ask Him to fortify you and to continue that good work in your life.

Notes
1. *The Spirit-Filled Bible* (Nashville, TN: Thomas Nelson Publishers, 1991), p. 1097.
2. James Strong, *The New Strong's Concordance of the Bible* (Nashville, TN: Thomas Nelson Publishers, 1990), ref. no. 3427.
3. Francis Brown, S. R. Driver, and Charles A. Briggs, *The New Brown-Driver, Briggs-Gesenius Hebrew and English Lexicon* (Peabody, MA: Hendrickson Publishers, 1979), p. 533.
4. Ethelbert W. Bullinger, *A Critical Lexicon and Concordance to the English and Greek New Testament* (Grand Rapids, MI: Zondervan Publishing House, 1975), p. 804.

CHAPTER SEVEN

BUTTERFLIES, MICE, ELEPHANTS AND BULL'S-EYES

So far we learned that as intercessors, God wants to use us as go-betweens to re-present Jesus and to enforce His victory. We've learned that our prayers of intercession can set up meetings for others to experience reconciliation with God or freedom from the powers of darkness. We've learned that these prayers of intercession are based upon Jesus' work of intercession on the cross; bearing up and carrying away the burdens of others are doable because of what He has already done. And we've learned that through a consistent and obedient prayer life, we can set up protective boundaries that disallow the enemy's plans to take effect in our lives and the lives of those we pray for. Now what? Hmmm . . . how about butterflies?

Our Helper
(pages 100-103)

Before we can explain the butterflies, we need to lay some groundwork about the Holy Spirit's role as our Helper.

1. Write out John 14:26. Underline the word "Helper."

_____

_____

_____

_____

The Greek word for "Helper" in this verse is *parakletos*, which literally means "one called alongside to aid, help or support."[1] *The Amplified Bible* uses seven words to communicate the richness of the meaning of *parakletos*: "Comforter," "Counselor," "Helper," "Intercessor," "Advocate," "Strengthen-er" and "Standby." Reread John 14:26, substituting for the word "Helper" all seven words that describe how the Holy Spirit works with us.

2. Describe a specific time when the Holy Spirit worked in your life in each of these ways:

Comforter

_____

_____

_____

Counselor

_____

_____

_____

Helper

_____

_____

_____

Intercessor

_____

_____

_____

Advocate

_____

_____

_____

Strengthener

Standby

3. Looking at the ministry of the Holy Spirit as our Helper and Intercessor, read Romans 8:26-28. Write out verse 26 and underline the words "helps," "weakness" and "should."

Now, a few more definitions to cull the treasure buried in this astounding verse: The word "helps" is the Greek word *sunantilambanomai*. When you combine the definitions of each of its three main parts (*sun, anti* and *lambano*), it literally means "take hold of together with against."[2] *Sunantilambanomai* communicates the idea that by the Holy Spirit's praying the will of God for whatever roadblocks we are facing, the Holy Spirit takes hold of that situation together with us, adding His strength to ours (see p. 107).

The word "weakness" comes from the Greek word *astheneia* and means "without strength."[3] It communicates the idea of being unable to produce results. By ourselves we cannot produce anything of eternal value, especially in regard to prayer; we must have the Holy Spirit alongside to aid us. Our weakness is too pervasive to expect any profitable success apart from Him.

The last word is "should." It is a legal term in the original Greek, *dei*, meaning "that which is necessary, right or proper in the nature of a case; what one must do; that which is legally binding."[4] It is this word that Jesus used when He said that the woman who was bent over because of a spirit of infirmity *should* be set free. Because she was a daughter of Abraham, it was her covenantal right—something that was proper and binding (see Luke 13:16).

4. Sum up the meaning of each of these words:

Helps

_____

_____

_____

Weakness

_____

_____

_____

Should

_____

_____

_____

In Romans 8:26, the Lord is saying that when we are without ability to know what is proper or right in a given situation, the Holy Spirit will take hold together with us, helping us to intercede according to the will of God. Think about that for a moment. Intercessory prayer is not about our coming up with a solution and somehow making it happen; it is about leaning on the strength of *the* Intercessor and allowing Him to pray through us what He knows to be the right answer.

5. Write out Zechariah 4:6.

_____

_____

_____

How was the Lord going to accomplish the work He had shown the prophet Zechariah?

_____

_____

_____

How does this relate to Romans 8:26 and our study of intercessory prayer?

_____

_____

_____

The only way to truly pray effectively is through the Holy Spirit. When we don't know what to pray and our weakness precludes us from changing a situation for the better, He is there to empower us, to pray through us and to see the rightful extension of the kingdom of God.

6. The Holy Spirit wants to help us. Look up the following verses and write down how the Holy Spirit comes to our aid. (There may be more than one way in each passage.)

John 14:26

_____

_____

_____

John 16:13-15

_____

_____

_____

1 Corinthians 2:10-12

_____

_____

_____

miss because what is by chance for us is not to our Helper, the Holy Spirit. In fact, *paga* also means 'bull's-eye' "[6] (see p. 104).

The Butterfly Anointing
(pages 105-111)

This is where the butterflies come in (well, not literally). Have you ever watched a butterfly fly? It darts here and there, moving in short spurts from one place to another—not with anywhere near the precision of, say, a hummingbird. Using this as an analogy for prayer, like a butterfly flutters in a seemingly unintentional course but knows exactly where it is going, we can pray in the Spirit knowing that though we may feel left to hit the mark by chance, in reality, God is sovereignly guiding us to *the* place where His will can be accomplished. In spite of our weakness and our inability to always know what is proper and necessary, we can rely upon the help of the Holy Spirit to guide our prayers to the right end. Bull's-eye!

9. Describe a time when you were sovereignly guided to dynamic prayer but did not realize it at the moment. What happened? How did you see your prayers go from a butterfly to a bull's-eye?

10. How does this concept of "butterfly prayer" relate to John 14:26 and Romans 8:26, which speak of the help of the Holy Spirit?

11. Among other things, *paga* means "meeting," "boundary," "light upon by chance" and "bull's-eye." Explain how each of these meanings contributes to our understanding of intercessory prayer.

Sometimes we can go a long time without understanding what we're praying for; we simply have the burden to pray and we do so. Once again it is our perseverance and obedience to the Lord that will enable us to walk through to the other side.

12. Write out 1 Timothy 6:12.

_____

_____

_____

What fight are we to persevere in?

_____

_____

_____

13. How does faith affect answered prayer (see Matthew 21:21-22 and Mark 11:22-24)?

_____

_____

_____

Dutch relates the story of praying for his wife, who had a cyst on her ovary. He was impressed to take an hour each day and pray in the Spirit for her. He did not know exactly what he was praying, but he yielded to the Helper of intercession, who did. After a month, the cyst was entirely gone, and his wife did not have to undergo surgery. Of this miracle Dutch exclaims, "A 'taking hold of together with against' happened. A 'Bethel' happened. A 'lighting on' happened. A 'laying on' and 'bearing away' happened. A 'meeting' happened. An 'enforcing' happened. A 'representation' happened" (p. 110).

14. What miracle is God wanting you to persevere in prayer to see happen?

_____

_____

15. Do you believe that God wants to release the work of Jesus through your prayers? If so, how will this affect your prayer life?

_____

_____

_____

There are going to be many times when you will not know how to pray for specific situations. Decide right now to allow the Holy Spirit to help you. Give Him the opportunity to take hold together with *you*. Who knows what Bethel is waiting for you?

Notes
1. W. E. Vine, *The Expanded Vine's Expository Dictionary of New Testament Words* (Minneapolis, MN: Bethany House Publishers, 1984), p. 200.
2. James Strong, *The New Strong's Exhaustive Concordance of the Bible* (Nashville, TN: Thomas Nelson Publishers, 1990), ref. no. 4878.
3. Spiros Zodhiates, *Hebrew-Greek Key Study Bible—New American Standard*, rev. ed. (Chattanooga, TN: AMG Publishers, 1990), p. 1812.
4. Spiros Zodhiates, *The Complete Word Study Dictionary* (Iowa Falls, IA: Word Bible Publishers, 1992), p. 400.
5. Francis Brown, S. R. Driver, and Charles A. Briggs, *The New Brown-Driver, Briggs-Gesenius Hebrew and English Lexicon* (Peabody, MA: Hendrickson Publishers, 1979), p. 803.
6. Avi Mizrachi, personal conversation with author, Dallas, TX.

CHAPTER EIGHT

SUPERNATURAL CHILDBIRTH

Much of the focus of intercessory prayer is for the lost to be saved; that is, for those who are spiritually dead to be born again. In recent years, the Church has mobilized in prayer specifically for the nations located in the 10/40 Window, a region of the world located between 10 degrees and 40 degrees latitude north of the equator, stretching from North Africa to Japan and the Philippines, where the presence of the gospel is seemingly nonexistent and Christianity is forbidden.[1] And answers have come. Supernatural breakthrough has begun in many of these nations; and people are being made alive, both in body and in spirit, by the power of the Holy Spirit. But the lost are all around us, too. What about our friends, neighbors and family? Does the Bible give us a model for this type of intercession—prayer that brings new life to people, even nations?

Travail, What Is It?
(pages 114-120)

If the idea of intercessory prayer is scary to some people, then one aspect of it in particular must send shivers up their spines: travail. Travailing as it relates to prayer usually conjures up images of old women—prayer warriors—rocking back and forth and moaning in the back of the church. Mysterious. Inexplicable. It just happens to some people sometimes for some reasons.

1. What do you think "travailing in prayer" is?

_____

_____

_____

2. How has "travail" been explained in your church or Bible study groups?

_____

_____

_____

3. What is your general experience with this aspect of intercessory prayer?

_____

_____

_____

Travail is often described as a strong burden to pray, in which one is overcome with weeping, deep feelings of concern and an urgency to cry out to God on someone's behalf. The reason may or may not be understood by the person travailing, but the necessity of the burden compels fervent prayer. Travail is thought of as uncontrollable and infrequent (except to those blue-haired prayer warriors in the back row!).

Dutch describes a time in his childhood when he experienced this type of prayer. He was 9 or 10 years old at the time; and as he was going to bed, he felt a strong compulsion to pray for his aunt. He wept uncontrollably and prayed for her salvation until the burden lifted—about 30 minutes or so. The following Sunday, his aunt traveled a long distance, "coincidentally" showed up at church and rededicated her life to the Lord.

4. Have you ever felt compelled to pray like this for someone? What happened?

_____

_____

_____

5. If this type of prayer is so powerful, why is it so infrequent and misunderstood?

_____

_____

_____

Travail is not as mysterious as some people make it out to be; and it is an important, if not essential, part of intercession for the lost. Travail is not necessarily weird or strange, nor is it always packed full of inarticulate moans and groans. The focus of this chapter is a biblical understanding of travail and why it brings forth new life.

Unfortunately, most of the Church's misunderstandings about prayer exist because we judge what is happening spiritually by what we see naturally. But this is not a good measuring stick; and it can lead to, as Dutch says, "extremes, imbalanced teaching, wrong expectations and striving after the flesh" (p. 118). We should not approach any prayer, especially travail, in this way. Prayer is not about the outward "signs" such as weeping or loud groaning, but rather it is about what God is doing in the spiritual realm as we become His go-betweens.

Dutch explains, "In any spiritual release of power and anointing, the possibility of a physical manifestation always exists—that is biblical. People may weep. People may at times fall down under the power of God. People may laugh, perhaps hilariously. They may even appear drunk. Sometimes when God moves there is a physical manifestation; oftentimes there is not. But *we can never ever judge what is happening in the spirit by what we see in the natural*" (p. 119).

6. What types of physical manifestations of God's power have you seen? What happened as a result of the physical manifestations?

---

7. How have you seen God move powerfully without a physical manifestation of His power?

---

8. What is your experience with judging spiritual things by what is seen outwardly? Has this ever led to confusion or misunderstanding? How was it resolved?

_____

_____

_____

9. Do you agree with Dutch's statement that a physical manifestation may accompany a spiritual release of people but that we cannot judge what is happening in the spirit by what we can see in the natural? Why or why not?

_____

_____

_____

Because of the tendency to judge spiritual advancement by physical manifestations, most people associate travail with what happens physically (i.e., loud, uncontrollable weeping; deep, anguished wailing; etc.); and in doing so, they miss the point of the prayer altogether: Something is being born in the spirit. To rightly understand travail, it is imperative that we realize that physical manifestations are *not* the verification that God is moving or that someone is spiritual. The Word of God forms the only foundation for our understanding of God and His ways. So let's look at what His Word says.

The Birthing Prayer
(pages 120-126)

Simply stated, travail is prayer that brings forth new life. God chose the word "travail" to emphasize the spiritual power being released, not the physical phenomena that may accompany it. In other words, people can travail and never scream or groan. The result is the focal point.

10. Write out John 7:38. Underline the phrase "innermost being."

_____

_____

_____

The phrase "innermost being" comes from the Greek word *koilia*, which also means "womb."[2] This verse tells us that as believers, we have the privilege of being "wombs" from which the life of God can come forth. We don't create this life, we carry it; and through the power of the Holy Spirit, we release it into the world. This life is released as we travail in prayer.

11. How do you feel about being a womb that is full of God's life?

    _____

    _____

    _____

12. Why is it important to remember that we don't create this life but only carry it?

    _____

    _____

    _____

Dutch defines "travail" as "releasing the creative power or energy of the Holy Spirit into a situation to produce, create or give birth to something" (p. 134). Carefully read each of the following passages, which either directly mentions travailing (birthing) prayer, or its context and wording imply it; and answer the corresponding questions.

13. Read 1 Kings 18:41-45 and James 5:16-18. Describe Elijah's posture as he prayed.

    _____

    _____

    _____

    What happened as a result of Elijah's prayers?

    _____

    _____

    _____

    _____

What adjectives did James use to describe Elijah's prayer?

_____

_____

Elijah's prayer position was similar to that of a woman giving birth. We are meant to see that Elijah was actually in travailing, or birthing, prayer. The word "earnestly" in James 5:17 indicates that Elijah's prayer was an intense time of intercession.

14. Read Psalm 126:5-6. What is being sown?

_____

_____

What is being reaped?

_____

_____

Within the context of the entire psalm, these verses speak of Israel's prayers for restoration from captivity. They help us understand the principle of sowing prayers in order to reap answers. Weeping can be a prayer that is just as powerful as eloquent words or supplications.

15. Read Isaiah 66:7-8. What enabled Zion to bring forth her sons?

_____

_____

The Hebrew word for "travail" in verse 8 is *chuwl* and means "give birth to."[3] As the people of God labored in prayer, He brought new life to them by restoring their country to them.

16. Read John 11:33,35,38,41-44. What was Jesus' response to this situation (see vv. 33,35,38)?

_____

_____

What do you think the Father heard (see v. 41)?

_____

_____

_____

What happened as a result?

_____

_____

_____

Although the Bible doesn't say specifically what Jesus prayed, it doesn't seem unwarranted to think that He was travailing, in this case with deep and intense groans, to birth a miracle of new life for his friend Lazarus.

17. Read Matthew 26:36-39. What words are used to describe how Jesus was feeling that night in the garden of Gethsemane?

_____

_____

_____

Compare this passage with the prophecy about Jesus in Isaiah 53:11. What aspect of travail do you see described in these verses?

_____

_____

_____

Matthew 26:36-39 expresses the deep sorrow Jesus felt as He began the work of redemption. The travail of His soul was so great that He shed drops of blood (see Luke 22:44). The blood that Jesus would shed on the cross to purchase our forgiveness, bringing us new life (see Romans 5:9; Ephesians 1:7 and Hebrews 9:22), began in the garden of Gethsemane. Jesus wasn't sorrowful because He was working so hard, per se; rather, it was because He was laboring to bring forth salvation, the new birth, for us. It was a powerful, dynamic time of birthing prayer.

18. Read Romans 8:26-27. How does the Holy Spirit intercede for us?

_____

_____

_____

In whose will is this intercession made?

_____

_____

_____

Looking back at verses 22-25 of Romans 8, we see that the context of this passage is travail. Creation is groaning and suffering "the pains of childbirth" (v. 22). Why? So that the sons of God will be revealed; that is, liberated from bondage and brought into freedom (see vv. 19-21). Just like creation, we, too, travail for this new birth to occur; we earnestly pray for the consummation of the will of God on Earth.

19. Read Galatians 4:19. For what purpose was Paul travailing?

_____

_____

_____

What connection do you think travailing prayer has to spiritual growth?

_____

_____

_____

Dutch sums up some truths about travail with the following short statements. As you read each conclusion, decide whether or not you agree with it and see if you can support the conclusion using the Scripture passages previously quoted.

- The Holy Spirit is involved.
- Travail is associated with spiritual reproduction.

- Travail aids in the maturing process of believers.
- Travail can be very intense, involving fervency, tears and even groaning.
- Travail is involved in producing physical miracles, not just the new birth.

20. How would you now define "travailing prayer"? How is it different from other types of intercession?

_____

_____

_____

What is produced by this kind of intercession?

_____

_____

_____

21. In what ways has travailing prayer brought forth new life to you or to someone you prayed for?

_____

_____

_____

22. Do you think that travailing prayer is something that is only initiated by the Holy Spirit, or do you think that it is something we can do at any time? Why?

_____

_____

_____

In your opinion, what part does the Holy Spirit play in travailing prayer? Upon what do you base this opinion?

_____

_____

_____

The Holy Spirit, God's Birthing Agent
(pages 126-137)

That last question leads us directly into this next part of the study. Though we travail in prayer, we do not birth anything ourselves—it is only through the power of the Holy Spirit in us that living water flows out of our innermost being.

23. Look up the following verses and jot down a brief summary about the work of the Holy Spirit that is being described:

Genesis 1:1-2

_____

_____

_____

Job 33:4

_____

_____

_____

Psalm 104:30 and Isaiah 32:15

_____

_____

_____

Luke 1:34-35

_____

_____

_____

Luke 4:14,18 and Acts 10:38

_____

_____

_____

John 3:3-8 and Titus 3:5-6

_____

_____

_____

Acts 1:8

_____

_____

_____

Acts 2:1-4

_____

_____

_____

As you can see from these Scriptures, the Holy Spirit is the One who brings about new life; He is the birthing agent of the Godhead. He is the active power behind the creation. He is the One who renews us and gives life to the will of God. Therefore, if we are going to accomplish anything in prayer, it must be because of His power working through us. Let's look more deeply at a few of these passages to determine how the Holy Spirit brings forth this new life through travailing praying.

24. From the *King James Version* of the Bible, copy Genesis 1:1-2 here. Underline the phrase "without form" and the word "moved."

_____

_____

_____

The Hebrew word for "without form" is *tohuw* and means "a desolation; to lie waste; a desert; empty (barren); a formless, lifeless mass."[4] In other words, the earth was totally lifeless. But the Holy Spirit moved over the barrenness. The Hebrew word translated as "moved" in this verse is *rachaph*, and it literally means "to brood over."[5] A brood is the offspring of something, that which is bred or produced. *Rachaph* is a reproductive term and is also used to describe a husband hovering over his bride. As the Spirit of God hovered over the earth, He was causing life to come forth on it.

25. Write out Psalm 90:2, remembering the Holy Spirit's work as an agent of creation. Underline the phrases "were born" and "give birth."

---

26. Reread Genesis 1:2. What new perspective does Psalm 90:2 bring to your understanding of the creation account in Genesis 1:2?

How does this description of creation relate to travailing, or birthing, prayer?

---

27. Read Deuteronomy 32:10-11,18, a passage about God's leading the children of Israel from Egypt into the land that He would give them to inhabit. How is the land described in verse 10?

In verse 11, what simile is used to explain the way the Lord cared for His people? How does this resonate with the other passages in this section of the study?

What travailing words are used in verse 18 to describe the Lord's relation to Israel?

_____

_____

How does this connect to our study of travail? Just as the Holy Spirit "brought forth" or "gave birth" to the earth, He wants to bring forth sons and daughters for the kingdom of God through our prayers. The hovering that once brought forth natural Israel will today bring forth spiritual Israel. Dutch says it this way: "He wants to go forth and hover around individuals, releasing His awesome power to convict, break bondages, bring revelation and draw them to Himself in order to cause the new birth or new creation in them. Yes, *the Holy Spirit wants to birth through us*" (p. 129).

28. Do you agree with Dutch's statement? Why or why not?

_____

_____

What does hovering have to do with new birth?

_____

_____

29. Have you seen the Holy Spirit "hover" over someone to bring new life to him or her? What happened?

_____

_____

30. Have you ever experienced the Holy Spirit "hovering" over you? What happened?

_____

_____

31. In what current situations do you think God wants to use you to bring forth new life through intercessory prayer?

_____

_____

_____

_____

Bringing Forth the Fruit of Calvary
(pages 137-141)

Acts 5:15 tells us of an amazing testimony to the Lord's desire to use His people in this area of intercession. It says that people were actually healed by coming under Peter's shadow. We know that it wasn't Peter himself who brought life back to these sickly bodies, but rather healing came by means of the hovering presence of the Holy Spirit at work through him. It was His shadow, His life-giving presence.

32. In light of the ideas presented in this lesson, explain why you agree or disagree with each of the following statements. If possible, describe a time when He used you in each way mentioned.

    Just as the Holy Spirit brought life at the creation, He wants to bring forth new creations through our intercession.

_____

_____

_____

_____

    Just as He hovered over the barren bodies of Abraham and Sarah to bring forth a new nation, Israel (see Genesis 21:1-2), He wants to bring forth a spiritual Israel from us through our intercession.

_____

_____

_____

_____

Just as He hovered over Mary to bring forth Christ in her (see Luke 1:35), He desires to use our travail to bring forth Christ in others.

Just as through Jesus' intercession Lazarus was raised from the dead (see John 11:43), the Holy Spirit wants to use us to bring forth spiritual life from death through our intercession.

Just as Jesus travailed for redemption in the garden of Gethsemane (see Matthew 26:39), the Holy Spirit wants to press forth the fruit of that redemption in our lives and the lives of others through our intercession.

Just as Peter's shadow brought healing (see Acts 5:15), the Holy Spirit wants to use us to overshadow others with His healing power through our intercession.

Let's take another look at Elijah's prayers. There is so much we learn from his experience of travailing prayer, recorded in 1 Kings 18. One of the most important truths from which we can learn is this: Even though it was the will of God that it rain, someone on Earth had to birth the rain through prayer. Dutch sums this up by saying, "Our prayers can and do cause the Holy Spirit to move into situations where

He then releases His power to bring life. We do have a part in producing the hovering of the Holy Spirit. The power that created the universe through His 'rachaph-ing' has been deposited in the Church—while untold millions await their births into the kingdom of God" (p. 140).

33. Comment on Dutch's conclusion. How does it affect your understanding of praying for the lost?

34. How has your understanding of travailing, or birthing, prayer changed?

35. How will your prayers of intercession be affected by this new understanding?

Notes
1. C. Peter Wagner, *Confronting the Powers* (Ventura, CA: Regal Books, 1996), p. 28.
2. W. E. Vine, *The Expanded Vine's Expository Dictionary of New Testament Words* (Minneapolis, MN: Bethany House Publishers, 1984), p. 110.
3. James Strong, *The New Strong's Exhaustive Concordance of the Bible* (Nashville, TN: Thomas Nelson Publishers, 1990), ref. no. 2342.
4. Ibid., ref. no. 8414; C. F. Keil and F. Delitzsch, *Commentary on the Old Testament, Volume 1* (Grand Rapids, MI: William B. Eerdmans Publishing, 1991), p. 48.
5. William Wilson, *Old Testament Word Studies* (Grand Rapids, MI: Kregel Publications, 1978), p. 175.

CHAPTER NINE

PRO WRESTLERS

By now you probably can recite by heart the two main aspects of intercession: reconciling and separating. Through prayer we stand as go-betweens to see people brought to God (reconciliation) to experience wholeness and restoration and to see people released from the powers of darkness (separation) to enjoy freedom and liberty in Christ. To see the full fruit of God's will established requires both aspects of intercessory prayer. In this chapter we will focus on the separating aspect in what has come to be known as spiritual warfare.

Paga Involves Warfare
(pages 145-151)

Unfortunately, many people do not believe in spiritual warfare. They feel that Jesus took care of the devil, so we don't need to concern ourselves with him.

1. In your understanding, in what way are we called to address evil spirits through prayer?

   _____

   _____

   _____

2. Is it biblical to command or rebuke demons?

   _____

   _____

3. What does it mean to "bind the devil"? Is binding the devil necessary in light of what Jesus did to defeat him?

_____

_____

_____

_____

This lesson is not meant to be a full explanation of the how-tos of spiritual warfare. Rather, the goal is to establish the decided connection
between spiritual warfare and intercession. To do this, let's go back to
the Hebrew word for intercession: *paga*. As we saw in chapter 4, there is
an inherent understanding of warfare in this tiny word. *Paga* is used 15
times to describe people meeting in battle.[1] It is translated as "attack,"
"fall upon," "strike down," "impinge" and other violent terms (see
Judges 8:21; 1 Samuel 22:11-19 and 2 Samuel 1:11-16 as examples).
There's no way around it: *paga* involves warfare. Trying to separate warfare from intercession is not only unbiblical but also detrimental.
Sometimes the root of a problem is spiritual and must be addressed
spiritually if breakthrough is going to happen.

4. Write out Ephesians 6:12.

_____

_____

_____

Against whom do we struggle?

_____

_____

_____

5. How has spiritual warfare been a part of your prayer life?

_____

_____

_____

_____

6. Describe a time when you tried, with natural means, to address a recurring problem that was rooted in a spiritual attack. What happened? Did spiritual warfare eventually play a part in seeing that attack cease? How?

_____

_____

_____

_____

This is not to imply that we should become demon hunters and assume that everything that goes wrong is because the devil is working against us or against the person we're praying for. Nor should we ignore our enemy, because ignoring him does not make him go away. In fact, ignorance in this area can be very costly.

7. Write out 2 Corinthians 2:11. Underline the words "advantage," "ignorant" and "schemes."

_____

_____

_____

_____

Though in context this verse is about forgiveness, a closer look at it helps us realize the necessity of understanding the validity of spiritual warfare and why ignorance of it can hurt us. The Greek word for "take advantage" in this verse is *pleonekteo* and literally means "to have or hold the greater portion" or to "overreach."[2] It connotes being taken advantage of by someone, letting that person have the greater part—the upper hand, if you will—in a situation. The word "ignorant" comes from the Greek word *agnoeo*, from which we derive our English word "agnostic." *Agnoeo* means "without knowledge or understanding."[3] The word "schemes" is *noema* and literally means "thought."[4] It implies plans, schemes, plots or devices because all of these are born in thought. Plainly stated, the verse says that we should not be without knowledge regarding the schemes of the devil, our enemy.

8. Rewrite 2 Corinthians 2:11, inserting the above definitions in place of the underlined words.

Dutch puts the definitions together this way: "To the degree we are ignorant of the way our adversary thinks and operates—of his plans, plots, schemes and devices—to that degree he will gain on us, prey on us, defraud us of what is ours and have or hold the greater portion" (p. 147).

9. How does your paraphrase compare with his?

10. Do you agree that ignorance of Satan's plans can be costly? Why or why not?

11. In what ways has ignorance of Satan's plans allowed him a "greater portion" in your life? In the lives of people that you know? In our society at large?

12. Compare Acts 16:7 with 1 Thessalonians 2:18. Are all hindrances necessarily demonic? How can you tell the difference? What does this have to do with being unaware of the devil's plans?

13. Do you think that all the trials that people face are because God allows them? In what sense does God allow everything that happens on this earth?

Dutch tells the story of a young man who had a history of instability in his life. This young man continually fluctuated between employment and unemployment, and between walking with the Lord and walking away from Him. During a time of prayer for this young man, the Lord revealed to the minister who was praying that three demons were following the young man, influencing him for the worse and causing the repeated instability. The minister bound the demonic spirits in Jesus' name, and then things began to dramatically change for the young man. He was able to pull his life together and eventually became a wealthy businessman. Dutch uses this example to show that though it is always right and good to ask God to strengthen and mature individuals, sometimes it is not enough. We need to engage in spiritual warfare to see the plans of the enemy exposed and nullified. Satan had the advantage as long as his plans remained hidden.

14. Do you know someone like this young man who, despite a personal desire to succeed and the support received from others, cannot seem to overcome his instabilities? How may ignorance of Satan's schemes be playing a part in this ongoing struggle?

---

15. Are there any destructive cycles in your own life that may be a result of a hidden plan of the enemy? How can you become aware of his schemes so that you are not taken advantage of?

---

16. Dutch makes the following general statements about spiritual warfare. Read each one together with the supporting Scripture passages. (Don't get lazy, now—look up the verses!)

   • We are in a very real war (see 2 Corinthians 10:4 and 1 Timothy 1:18).
   • We are soldiers in this war (see Psalm 110:2-3 and 2 Timothy 2:3-4).
   • We are to wrestle against all levels of the kingdom of darkness (see Ephesians 6:12).
   • We are to resist the devil (which, in most situations, would be his demons), and he will flee from us (see James 4:7 and 1 Peter 5:9).
   • We are to tread on Satan and his demons (i.e., exercise authority over them—see Luke 10:19 and Romans 16:20).
   • We are to cast out demons (see Mark 16:17).
   • We have authority to bind (forbid) and loose (permit) when dealing with agents and gates of hell (see Matthew 16:19).
   • We have powerful weapons designed to overcome the kingdom of darkness (see 2 Corinthians 10:4 and Ephesians 6:10-20).

   In light of these statements and supporting Bible verses, what are your thoughts now about spiritual warfare?

   _____

   _____

   _____

17. How would you respond to those who do not believe in spiritual warfare?

   _____

   _____

   _____

Notice that the Bible does not give us a formula for prayer of this type. That's because there is none. God is a God of relationship, not formulas. Spiritual warfare isn't our beating up the devil in three easy steps. It's our being in union with the Lord of the universe and following His instructions according to His timing to deal with the enemy. Warfare—actually, *everything* good and right—flows out of our devotion to Him.

Devotion to Christ, the Springboard for Everything
(pages 151-155)

Dutch makes the statement, *"Out of our waiting often comes warring"* (p. 151). This goes along with the definition of intercession as standing in-between. We must have that connection with God before we can reach out to help others through intercessory prayer—and this means we must learn to *wait* on the Lord. Let's consider three Hebrew words that teach us about waiting on God.

The first Hebrew word used for the idea of waiting is *dumiyah*. It is found in Psalm 62:1 and conveys the idea of silently waiting with a quiet trust.[5]

18. Write out Psalm 62:1-2.

19. Write out Psalm 33:20.

The word "wait" in this verse is *chakah* and means "to adhere to" or "long for."[6] It implies a deep desire for something or someone.

20. Write out Isaiah 40:31.

"Wait" in this verse comes from the Hebrew word *qavah* and means "to wait with eager expectation" or "to bind something together by twisting."[7] The main idea behind this word is expectation and oneness.

These three Hebrew words help us define what it means to wait on the Lord, to have pure devotion for Him. We are to wait in silent trust, longing for and eagerly expecting His presence. Then we will enjoy oneness with Him as our hearts become entwined with His.

21. How would you describe your devotion to the Lord?

_____

_____

22. In what ways do you trust, adhere to, long for and eagerly expect the Lord? How are these things strengthened in your life?

_____

_____

_____

23. Read Psalm 37:7,9,34. What is the relationship between waiting on the Lord and inheriting what He has promised? How does this demonstrate the connection between worship and warfare?

_____

_____

_____

24. Read Luke 10:38-42. What did Jesus mean when He said that Mary chose "the good part" (v. 42)?

_____

_____

What is the difference between devotion to the Lord and service for the Lord?

_____

_____

How have you experienced both being a Martha and being a Mary?

_____

_____

_____

To sum this up, "We must wait in His presence and allow all ministry, including our warfare, to be born of relationship" (p. 155). Do you agree? Why or why not?

_____

_____

_____

God's Timing, God's Terms, God's Method
(pages 155-159)

Waiting upon the Lord will keep us from becoming reactionary to the enemy. Spiritual warfare is not a response to the devil. It is a God-guided, God-timed battle. We follow our Captain, not our foe.

25. Have you ever reacted to a spiritual attack instead of first waiting on the Lord for His instructions? What happened?

_____

_____

_____

26. Read Joshua 6. What battle plan did God give Joshua for defeating Jericho?

_____

_____

_____

What was His timing for its defeat?

_____

_____

_____

What were His terms regarding prisoners?

_____

_____

_____

27. Read 2 Samuel 5:24. When were David and his men to attack the Philistines?

_____

_____

_____

28. Read 1 Samuel 13:8-14. What time had Samuel set for offering the sacrifice?

_____

_____

_____

What did Saul do?

_____

_____

_____

What resulted?

_____

_____

_____

29. Read 2 Chronicles 20:1-30 and Acts 16:16-36. How did God send victory to His people in each of these situations? In other words, what method did He have them use to deliver them from their troubles?

_____

_____

_____

30. From these five examples, how can we see that there is no formula for spiritual warfare?

Sometimes the Lord instructs us to shout. Other times He tells us to love, weep or worship. The method is not a cookie-cutter answer for all our battles. We must be people who, above all things, seek ongoing fellowship with the Lord we love.

31. Describe some of the methods, or strategies, the Holy Spirit has given to you to war against the enemy.

32. How does the truth that there is no formula for spiritual warfare underscore the need for us to have an ongoing devotion to Christ if we are going to intercede for others?

Seizing and Securing Our Inheritance
(pages 159-166)

Dutch makes the point, "Remember we are not trying to defeat the devil. He is already defeated. We do not re-defeat, we re-present, the victory of the Cross" (pp. 159-160). Jesus shattered the headship of the serpent (see Genesis 3:15 and Psalm 2:9), the devil; and as His representatives, we must release and enforce the victory.

Just as the children of Israel had to fight for the Promised Land, though it was already theirs by God's decree, we must take hold of the inheritance we have received in Christ—and we do this through prayer that rises out of devotion to Him.

33. Write out 1 Timothy 6:12.

_____

_____

What are we to take hold of? Don't we already possess it?

_____

_____

How can we take hold of our spiritual inheritance?

_____

_____

What do you think this verse is saying? How does it relate to prayer?

_____

_____

_____

We must seize what is rightfully ours. From God? No! From the world, the flesh and the devil—from whatever is seeking to bar us from receiving God's blessing. Why can we do this? Because when Jesus defeated the devil, it was a complete disarmament. The devil's authority was dissolved (see 1 John 3:8). Dutch explains, *"Power never was and never will be the issue between God and Satan. Authority was the issue—the authority Satan had obtained through Adam"* (p. 163). This puts into proper perspective our role in spiritual warfare. We are not reconquering the devil; we are acting in the authority Jesus gave to us to enforce the victory He already won.

34. Read Exodus 17:8-13. What happened during the battle when Moses held up his staff?

_____

_____

_____

The Israelite victory described in this passage was decided not by the strength of the army but by the raising of the staff, which represented the authority of God.

35. What is the difference between authority and power?

How does this relate to spiritual warfare?

36. Write out Colossians 1:13.

From what has God delivered us?

37. Write out Luke 10:19.

Over what has He given us authority?

38. To review, what exactly are we doing in spiritual warfare? Why is spiritual warfare even possible?

_____

_____

_____

39. What areas of your inheritance do you need to secure?

_____

_____

_____

In conclusion, *"There is a warfare or wrestling that is necessary at times in our intercession. Paga* includes the concept and the Scriptures teach it. We must do it with balance and understanding, but *we must do it*! To ignore Satan is to abdicate to Satan"* (p. 166). Just like pro wrestlers possess great strength to defeat their adversaries, we, too, have been given all the authority we need to step forward and face the powers of darkness. The starting bell has rung—go for it!

Notes
1. R. Laird Harris, Gleason L. Archer, Jr., and Bruce K. Waltke, *Theological Wordbook of the Old Testament*, rev. ed. (Grand Rapids, MI: William B. Eerdmans Publishing, 1991), p. 715.
2. Spiros Zodhiates, *The Complete Word Study Dictionary* (Iowa Falls, IA: Word Bible Publishers, 1992), p. 1173; James Strong, *The New Strong's Exhaustive Concordance of the Bible* (Nashville, TN: Thomas Nelson Publishers, 1990), ref. no. 4122.
3. Ethelbert W. Bullinger, *A Critical Lexicon and Concordance to the English and Greek New Testament* (Grand Rapids, MI: Zondervan Publishing House, 1975), p. 400.
4. Spiros Zodhiates, *Hebrew-Greek Key Study Bible—New American Standard*, rev. ed. (Chattanooga, TN: AMG Publishers, 1990), p. 1797.
5. James Strong, *The New Strong's Exhaustive Concordance of the Bible* (Nashville, TN: Thomas Nelson Publishers, 1990), ref. no. 1747.
6. Ibid., ref. no. 2442.
7. Harris, Archer, Waltke, *Theological Wordbook*, p. 791; Strong, *The New Strong's Exhaustive Concordance*, ref. no. 6960.

CHAPTER TEN

MOST HIGH MAN

In the last chapter, we established the validity and necessity of spiritual warfare. Now we will focus on how this warfare relates to praying for the lost. Think about your own circle of friends, family and acquaintances. How many of them are still lost in sin, separated from the God who created them and loves them? Is there anything we can do, as those who are called to re-present Jesus, to see them delivered from darkness and brought into the kingdom of God? Yes, there is!

Peeling Off the Veils
(pages 168-172)

Have you ever played Pin the Tail on the Donkey? Someone blindfolds you, spins you around a little and sets you off to accurately pin a paper tail on a seemingly nowhere-to-be-found poster of a donkey. Those watching laugh as you ineptly stumble across the room; and you aren't positive, but you think that the donkey is laughing, too. Inevitably (if you haven't managed to peek through the blindfold), you pin the tail on a random and definitely erroneous location such as the neighbor's back-porch door. It's a funny—well, at least mildly amusing—game.

On a much more serious note, there is a blindfold—a veil—that keeps unbelievers from clearly seeing the gospel. And if they continue in their aimless, unguided pursuit, they will spend eternity without Christ.

1. Write out 2 Corinthians 4:3-4. Underline each instance of the word "veiled."

_____

_____

_____

_____

The Greek word for "veil" is *kalupsis* and means "to hide, cover up, wrap around."[1] Examples of this veiling are the bark that veils the inside of a tree or the skin that veils the inside of a body. The opposite of this word is *apokalupsis*. The prefix *apo-* means "off or away."[2] *Apokalupsis* is translated as the word "revelation," indicating that the veil that had hidden something has now been taken off.

The verses in 2 Corinthians 4 do not tell us that unbelievers *won't* see the gospel but that they *can't*. They don't understand the truth of it because they are blinded to it. The point of this chapter is that we have a part to play in seeing that veil taken off. We participate in the destruction of the forces that blind the minds of unbelievers. How? Intercessory prayer! Through spiritual warfare, we can demolish the strongholds that have held the lost captive.

2. Describe a time when you had difficulty understanding why someone didn't accept the gospel when it was clearly and powerfully presented.

_____

_____

_____

According to 2 Corinthians 4:3-4, why shouldn't this have surprised you?

_____

_____

_____

3. In your own salvation experience, when did you first see Christ clearly? Can you pinpoint a time when you sensed that the blindfold had come off?

_____

_____

_____

Go back to question 1 and underline the word "light" in 2 Corinthians 4:4. This comes from the Greek word *photismos*, which means "illumination."[3] When we illuminate something, we let in the light. In fact, our English word "photograph" is derived from this Greek word. Think about this for a moment: What happens when you take a photograph? The camera shutter opens to let in light, and the result is a picture. If the shutter fails to open, then no light comes in and no picture is made. Can you see how this relates to someone's seeing the gospel? No matter how majestic and powerful the message is, if the veil has not been removed (if the shutter has not been opened), there is no ability to see Jesus clearly.

4. Some statistics claim that fewer than 10 percent of the people who "get saved" in America become true followers of Christ. Why do you think this happens?

_____

_____

_____

_____

5. What is your personal experience with seeing someone pray to receive Christ, and then seeing that he or she never really walks with Him or shows fruit of His work in his or her life? Why do you think this happened?

_____

_____

_____

6. Why isn't praying a salvation prayer enough?

_____

_____

_____

7. Read Acts 26:17-18. Notice the sequence described in this verse: open, turn, receive. How does this relate to someone's experiencing true salvation?

_____

_____

_____

Salvation follows repentance, and repentance comes through revelation. Saying a salvation prayer without a true revelation, or unveiling, of who Jesus is, is not truly experiencing salvation. This is why so many people who make a decision for Christ never follow through. The veil was never removed, and they did not really see Him.

Information Versus Revelation
(pages 172-174)

Our culture values information. Consider the numerous ways in which we receive it: Internet, newspapers, TV, radio, books, magazines, movies, etc. If we want to, we can engage in a continuous stream of knowledge—some helpful but most not. The problem is that we tend to approach acquiring spiritual truth as we would any other subject of interest: through the mind. Dutch explains, "Information is of the mind; biblical revelation, however, involves and affects the mind, but originates from the heart" (p. 172).

8. In your understanding, what is the difference between knowledge and revelation?

_____

_____

_____

How does this affect someone's spiritual understanding?

_____

_____

_____

_____

9. When have you "known" something for years only to one day awake to a true revelation of it?

_____

_____

_____

Information does not automatically equal revelation, and it does not always result in salvation. People can know a lot about the Bible but never experience its power. Consider the example of the Pharisees whom Jesus addresses in John 5:39.

10. Read John 5:39. What were the Pharisees diligent to do?

_____

_____

_____

To what did Jesus say that the Scriptures were pointing?

_____

_____

_____

Why do you think that the Pharisees failed to move from information about Him to revelation of who He truly was?

_____

_____

_____

11. Read 1 Corinthians 2:14. Without the Spirit, what will the natural man think about God and His ways?

_____

_____

_____

_____

Apart from revelation, knowledge remains simply information. It takes the power of the Holy Spirit to unveil the truth and allow people to see it clearly. By simply appealing to the intellect in our effort to share the gospel, we shortcut the process and short-circuit the results.

Birthing True Repentance
(pages 174-177)

So what do we do about this? Dutch says, "We must allow the Holy Spirit time to birth true repentance in [the lost] through God-given revelation" (p. 174). And this is where we come in. Obviously, we cannot take God's place in actually bringing revelation of His truth to other people; but we can step in and, through spiritual warfare, take off the blindfold so that in His perfect timing, they can clearly see what He longs for them to see: a picture of Himself greeting them with open arms and exuberant joy.

It starts, however, with us. We must have "clean hands and a pure heart" (see Psalm 24:3-4). Harboring unforgiveness or bitterness will hinder our prayers from being heard (see Mark 11:25-26). And Jesus instructs us to take the log out of our own eye so that we can see clearly to take the speck out of someone else's eye (see Matthew 7:5).

12. Has unforgiveness ever hindered your prayers? When did you realize it? What did you do about it?

_____

_____

_____

_____

13. Why is it so important that an intercessor have "clean hands and a pure heart" as far as they know?

_____

_____

_____

_____

Take a moment to reflectively search your heart. Ask the Holy Spirit to show you any areas of unforgiveness that you need to address right now. As He does, choose to forgive and let Him cleanse and heal any wounds. As intercessors, we must stand before God having dealt with the areas of unforgiveness that He has shown us need to be dealt with.

Once we are ready ourselves, we can battle for others. How does Satan blind the minds of unbelievers? Look back at 2 Corinthians 4:4. The word "blinded" is the Greek word *tuphloo* and means "to dull the intellect; to make blind."[4] In this passage, blindness is like a smoke screen, which prevents people from seeing clearly. From the root word of *tuphloo* comes another word that is used to describe something that is proud, high-minded or inflated with self-conceit.[5] The idea is that of something being "puffed up," much like smoke, which billows when it rises. Putting these definitions in context, we can see that Satan uses pride to blind unbelievers. The same sin that caused the fall of humanity continues to cause people to live as enemies of God.

14. In your own words, describe how pride can blind us to truth.

_____

_____

_____

How have you experienced this personally?

_____

_____

_____

How does this relate to a person's spiritual life?

_____

_____

_____

15. Some say that pride is stronger in men than in women. Do you believe this is true? Why or why not?

_____

_____

_____

16. How does understanding the blinding ability of pride aid us in praying for the lost?

_____

_____

_____

Praying for the Lost
(pages 178-183)

God has not left us without a solution to the pride problem. In fact, He gives us powerful and certain ways to deal with it.

17. Write out 2 Corinthians 10:3-5.

_____

_____

_____

What does it mean that our weapons are not "of the flesh," or not "of the world" (*NIV*)?

_____

_____

_____

_____

How does this relate to the idea that intellectual reasoning alone won't bring revelation?

_____

_____

_____

What can our weapons demolish?

_____

_____

_____

What can our weapons take captive?

_____

_____

_____

Read this passage in 2 Corinthians 10:3-5 as it is paraphrased in *The Living Bible*:

> It is true that I am an ordinary, weak human being, but I don't use human plans and methods to win my battles. I use God's mighty weapons, not those made by men, to knock down the devil's strongholds. These weapons can break down every proud argument against God and every wall that can be built to keep men from finding him. With these weapons I can capture rebels and bring them back to God, and change them into men whose hearts' desire is obedience to Christ.

Look back at 2 Corinthians 10:4 and underline the word "powerful." This is the Greek word *dunatos* and is actually one of the New Testament words for "miracle."[6] We get our English word "dynamite" from it. In other words, the power that God has given to us as a weapon against Satan is nothing less than spiritual dynamite. What are we to blow up with this holy charge? The strongholds, or fortresses, of the enemy. The word "demolish" in verse 5 (*NIV*) is the Greek word *kathairesis* and means "to bring down with violence or demolish."[7] Every time we pray for someone who is blinded to truth, we lay another blow against what holds him or her in bondage. If we persist in prayer, the stronghold *will* fall.

The Stronghold, Satan's Prison Within
(pages 183-189)

We've talked about demolishing strongholds through spiritual warfare, especially those strongholds that blind the minds of unbelievers. But what exactly is a stronghold? A stronghold is a place from which to hold something securely. It is like a fortress or a garrison built to contain and protect. A stronghold is not necessarily bad—only those that keep people locked away from truth are negative. And those are the ones that we've been given power to break down.

Exactly what are spiritual strongholds made of? To answer this, go back and reread—you guessed it—2 Corinthians 10:3-5. Verse 4 speaks of our ability to demolish a stronghold. Verse 5 then goes on to explain what a stronghold is made of. Reread this verse, noting the words "speculations," "lofty thing" and "thought." We'll look at each of these individually.

First, strongholds are comprised of "speculations"—human reasoning, wisdom or logic.[8] As we grow, we accumulate knowledge and wisdom from the world around us. From this we build a mindset, which becomes a filter for everything we hear. Philosophies, belief systems and worldviews are all mindsets that we deal with on a daily basis.

18. Explain how a mindset becomes a filter for everything one hears.

_____

_____

_____

In what ways can a mindset blind someone?

_____

_____

_____

19. What mindsets held you before you came to Christ?

_____

_____

_____

20. How have you experienced the truth that divine weapons can demolish speculations?

_____

_____

_____

21. Who can you pray for right now in regard to this? Well, *pray!*

_____

_____

Second, a stronghold is comprised of "lofty" things. Other Bibles translate this as a "high thing" (*KJV*) and "pretension" (*NIV*). The Greek word for these phrases is *hupsoma* and means "any elevated place or thing."[9] Sound familiar? It refers to the same root of pride we read about in 2 Corinthians 4:3-4. A lofty thing, in the context of strongholds, is a claim or bold assertion that is put forward as truth; it is any idea or mindset that lifts itself above God. He is the Exalted One—the Most High God (see 2 Samuel 22:47 and Psalm 57:5). Nothing can be elevated higher than He is. Yet, in the blindness of pride, many lofty things often attempt to be.

22. Explain what a lofty thing is.

_____

_____

_____

_____

23. How do speculations and lofty things work together to create a stronghold?

_____

_____

24. What ideas or mindsets do you see lifted above God in our current culture? Why is it sometimes hard to identify them?

_____

_____

_____

25. What lofty thing, or bold claim, do you struggle against as you intercede for others?

_____

_____

_____

Third, strongholds are composed of thoughts. Not only are we to demolish speculations and high things, we are also told that our weapons can take every thought captive. This word for "thought" in 2 Corinthians 10:5 is the Greek word *noema*, which we discussed in the previous chapter. As you probably recall, it means plans, schemes, devices or plots. Dutch describes it in this way: "[*Noema*] refers to the spontaneous thoughts and temptations Satan uses to assault the unbelievers, as well as the schemes and plans he uses to keep them in darkness" (p. 187). Often this verse is quoted by believers in regard to their own thoughts—which is great! But the context of the passage makes it clear that we can also take captive the rebellious *noema* of the enemy so that others can respond to the power of the gospel.

26. According to verse 5, what is the purpose of taking these thoughts captive?

_____

_____

_____

27. In what ways have you seen specific thoughts, plans or schemes of the enemy hinder people from responding to the gospel?

_____

_____

_____

28. How do our prayers of intercession take these plans captive?

_____

_____

_____

29. Who do you know who needs to have spiritual strongholds (speculations and lofty things) demolished and rebellious plans taken captive so that they can come to Christ?

_____

_____

_____

_____

Take a moment and use your divine dynamite to lay some blows against the enemy right now. Commit to intercede on behalf of the people whose names you wrote down until those strongholds fall and your friends walk out into God's freedom.

30. Dutch concludes this topic with a spiritual warfare *noninclusive* checklist. Don't worry, it's *not* meant to be a formula—just a condensed group of truths that can play a part in prayer for the lost. Read the following statements and comment in the space below on how you can incorporate them into your personal times of prayer and warfare.

   • Pray that God would lift the veil (revelation and enlightenment).
   • Pray for the Holy Spirit to hover over them and protect them.
   • Cast down anything that would exalt itself against the knowledge of God, specifically pride and rebellion. (This is the *hupsoma* aspect of the stronghold.)
   • Take down all known strongholds—thought patterns, opinions on religion, materialism, fear.
   • Bind Satan from taking them captive. Bind all wicked thoughts and lies that would try to take hold in their minds.
   • Pray that the armor of God would be placed on them.

_____

_____

_____

_____

_____

_____

_____

_____

_____

_____

As representatives of Jesus, we are called to enforce and make effectual the freedom Christ pronounced. Unbelievers can't do this for themselves. They cannot overcome the strongholds of darkness, nor lift the veils on their own—they need help. And God has graced us with divine power to fight the enemy on their behalf. So, let's fight!

Let me reiterate that this chapter is not meant to be a thorough treatment of spiritual warfare for the lost. There are many great books on the topic; ask your pastor for his or her recommendation.

Notes

1. Spiros Zodhiates, *The Complete Word Study Dictionary* (Iowa Falls, IA: Word Bible Publishers, 1992), p. 816.
2. James Strong, *The New Strong's Exhaustive Concordance of the Bible* (Nashville, TN: Thomas Nelson Publishers, 1990), ref. no. 575.
3. Zodhiates, *The Complete Word Study Dictionary*, p. 1464.
4. W. E. Vine, *The Expanded Vine's Expository Dictionary of New Testament Words* (Minneapolis, MN: Bethany House Publishers, 1984), p. 125.
5. Strong, *The New Strong's Exhaustive Concordance of the Bible*, ref. no. 5187.
6. Ibid., ref. no. 1415.
7. Ibid., ref. no. 2507.
8. Zodhiates, *The Complete Word Study Dictionary*, p. 923.
9. Strong, *The New Strong's Exhaustive Concordance of the Bible*, ref. no. 5313.

CHAPTER ELEVEN

THE LIGHTNING OF GOD

One of the most powerful and awesome forces in nature is lightning. Lightning is the sudden release of the charge built upon millions of water particles within a thundercloud. A single bolt can reach 30,000 degrees Celsius (45,000 degrees Fahrenheit)—hotter than the surface of the sun—and can generate enough electricity to light 10 million homes for one month. Now that's a lot of power!

What does lightning have to do with intercession? Interestingly, *paga* can be translated as "to strike the mark."[1] This is seen in Job 36:32: "He covers His hands with the lightning, and commands it *to strike the mark*" (emphasis added). The picture this verse gives us is that of God holding lightning in His hands, releasing it to His desired target. And this release of power striking its mark is likened to intercession.

God Is Light
(pages 192-196)

In order to see the connection between lightning and intercession, it is necessary to lay down some groundwork from the Scriptures. Let's begin by looking at the Scriptures that describe the connection between God and light. This initial study will include a lot of reading and writing, but it will yield a rich understanding of God and His ways—so keep at it!

1. Write out 1 John 1:5. Underline the phrase "God is light."

_____

_____

_____

2. Read 1 Timothy 6:16. Where does God dwell?

_____

_____

3. Read Hebrews 1:3. Notice the phrase "radiance of His glory." *The Amplified Bible* expounds upon this phrase that describes Jesus as "the Light-being, the out-raying or radiance of the divine." How does this connect God and light?

_____

_____

_____

4. Read Exodus 19:16-17, James 1:17 and Revelation 4:5. What further connections do these verses make between God and light (or lightning)?

_____

_____

_____

Having established the fact that God is light, that in His very being He radiates a luminosity that is both tangible and powerful, let's look at how God's light and the release of it are associated with His glory.

5. Read Luke 2:9. What shone in the sky?

_____

_____

_____

6. Read Luke 9:29-32. How is Jesus' clothing described?

_____

_____

_____

What did the disciples see when they became fully awake?

_____

_____

_____

7. Read Revelation 21:23. What gives light to the New Jerusalem?

_____

_____

_____

8. In light of these passages, what is the connection between light and God's glory?

_____

_____

_____

As you can see from the above passages, the glory of God is frequently explained as the light that comes from God. His glory is an extension of Himself. At times it is released through His mouth and is often called a sword. First, let's consider some verses that establish the idea of God's Word (or mouth) as a sword, and then we'll make the connection between the sword and light (and lightning).

9. Read Ephesians 6:17 and Hebrews 4:12. To what is God's Word likened?

_____

_____

_____

_____

10. Read Revelation 2:16. How would Jesus fight against the people of the church in Pergamum who were following false teachings?

_____

_____

_____

11. Read Revelation 19:15. What comes out of His mouth? For what purpose?

_____

_____

_____

12. Read Psalms 18:13-14; 29:7; and Hosea 6:5. Notice the words "voice," "words," "light" and "lightning." How do these verses convey the idea of God's Word, or voice, being a weapon?

_____

_____

_____

Okay, let's recap: God is associated with light (or lightning), which sometimes shines forth as His glory. It is released by His Word and is likened to a powerful weapon—a sword. The last round of passages we will look at center on God's light in the context of His dealing with His enemies.

13. Read Psalms 77:17-18; 78:48; Ezekiel 21:9-10,15,28; and Revelation 8:5; 11:19; 16:18. Describe what happens when God's lightning is released.

_____

_____

_____

Without jumping to conjecture, it is within the bounds of balanced exegesis to suggest that in some of the above references the lightning was not apparent to the natural eye. Certainly some was, but in other cases, it may be that lightning was used as a word picture to describe what happened in the spiritual realm.

14. Why do you think God would choose to describe His glory and its release as lightning?

_____

_____

_____

15. Have you ever been near lightning when it struck the earth? What happened? What did you feel?

_____

_____

_____

_____

16. Can you identify a time when you experienced a similar feeling because of God's glory being revealed? Describe what happened.

_____

_____

_____

_____

17. What is the connection between lightning and intercession?

_____

_____

_____

Considering these passages as a whole, we can conclude that God is light and that at times this light flashes forth from Him as bolts of lightning. This lightning is often a blow to defeat an enemy and bring deliverance. When God's power strikes the mark—*paga*—His glory is released to accomplish His will. And this is the connection we can derive between the lightning of God and intercession. There is a place in prayer for seeing the glory of God strike the enemy and release the captives. We can release His power by speaking His Word.

Light Overcomes Darkness
(pages 196-202)

In Luke 10:18 we read that Jesus saw Satan "fall from heaven like lightning." God's judgment against Satan's sin of pride resulted in a bolt of lightning—literal or not, it makes no difference—that shot him out of God's presence. Light overcame darkness.

When Jesus came to Earth, He came as light. John 1:4-5 tells us that His light shone in our dark world and that the darkness could not overcome or conquer it. The most dramatic example of this was the defeat of Satan at the Cross. When the false angel of light met the God who is light, it was all over. There was no way for the darkness to prevail. God's light scattered the enemy forever.

Now this light lives in us. As followers of Christ, we have been lit up by His glory. We can stand in confidence against darkness, knowing that the same light that lives in Jesus—the glory of God—lives in us today.

18. Read Isaiah 60:1-3. What should we cause to arise and shine from us?

_____

_____

_____

_____

_____

19. Read Ephesians 5:8. What are believers called in this verse?

_____

_____

_____

_____

The light continues; the victory lives on. How? Through the Church! Dutch provides the following summary. Read it carefully and consider each statement.

> If intercession is pictured by God's lightning striking the mark . . . and if Christ's work of intercession when He met Satan, breaking his headship, was light overcoming darkness . . . and if our praying intercession simply releases or re-presents Christ's . . . then I think it safe to say that our intercession releases the lightning of God to flash forth into situations, bringing devastation to the powers of darkness (p. 199).

20. Do you agree with this conclusion? Why or why not?

_____

_____

_____

Dutch refers to a time during a ministry outreach when God intervened to calm a potentially violent man. Though Dutch and his team did not address the man themselves, they prayed and then watched as the antagonistic man went from being aggressive to retreating in confusion. He recalls, "His countenance changed, his voice changed and his attitude changed. The demons controlling him had been overcome. Light prevailed" (p. 202).

21. Describe a time when you saw God's glory released into a situation because of intercession.

_____

_____

_____

22. How is it biblical to say that the light the Church is called to shine includes intercession to "strike the mark" of the enemy?

_____

_____

_____

Living Temples That Carry Glory
(pages 202-205)

Here's where the rubber meets the road and why we can intercede for the lightning of God to dispel the enemy and release his captives.

In the Old Testament, God's presence—His light and glory—dwelt among His people. As believers, we are filled with the very light and glory of God. Go back and reread that last sentence aloud—*slowly*. The very light and glory of God—amazing, isn't it? We are temples of the one true and living God. He dwells in us by His Spirit.

23. Write out 1 Corinthians 3:16. Underline the words "temple" and "dwells."

_____

_____

_____

The word "temple" in this passage is the Greek word *naos*, which always referred to the holy of holies—that inner room of the Temple in which the presence of God dwelled.[2] "Dwells" comes from the Old Testament word *shakan*, from which we get the word "shekinah."[3] The "shekinah glory" was the abiding, or dwelling, glory of the holy of holies. What does this mean to us today? We are the new holy of holies, the place where God's glory lives.

24. Write out 2 Corinthians 4:6-7.

_____

_____

_____

What treasure is described in this verse? Where does it dwell?

_____

_____

_____

How do these verses reaffirm your confidence as an intercessor?

_____

_____

_____

Going back to the Old Testament, we see that Israel carried the Ark of the Covenant into battle (see Joshua 6:6-7). The Ark represented God's presence and contained three things: manna, Aaron's rod and the stone tablets that contained the Ten Commandments (see Hebrews 9:4). Though it's outside of the scope of this study to develop the symbolism found in each of these items, one aspect of the Ark's use in battle is important for us to consider here. As the Ark was carried out into battle, the people would cry, "Rise up, O Lord! And let Thine enemies be scattered, and let those who hate Thee flee before Thee" (Numbers 10:35; see also Psalm 68:1). God's presence, His glory, went before the people to destroy their enemies. That same presence lives in believers today, and we—those in whom His glory dwells—carry His presence into battle and see the enemy put to flight, for ourselves as well as for others.

25. How do we, as temples of God, carry His presence into battle? What happens as a result?

_____

_____

_____

26. How does this relate to God, lightning and intercession?

_____

_____

Dutch ends by saying, "As the Israelites carried the presence and glory of God into battle, so must we. All that was in the Ark of the Covenant is in us: the Bread of Life, the rod of priestly authority and the law of God. And the glory that was upon it now shines through us. Act like it! Strike with the sword—speak the Word! 'Let God arise' through your intercession 'and His enemies be scattered'" (pp. 204-205).

27. What situations can you think of right now in which darkness needs to be scattered? How can the truths presented in this lesson help you pray? Take a moment and intercede, speaking the Word of God boldly so that His glory may be released and His light drive out that darkness.

_____

_____

_____

Notes
1. James Strong, *The New Strong's Exhaustive Concordance of the Bible* (Nashville, TN: Thomas Nelson Publishers, 1990), ref. no. 6293.
2. Joseph Henry Thayer, *A Greek-English Lexicon of the New Testament* (Grand Rapids, MI: Baker Book House, 1977), p. 422.
3. Strong, *The New Strong's Exhaustive Concordance of the Bible*, ref. no. 7931.

CHAPTER TWELVE

THE SUBSTANCE OF PRAYER

Fast food. Get rich quick. No-waiting home loans. Rapid weight loss. Instant Internet access. We live in a culture of the immediate. We want everything now. If we have to wait—or worse yet, work for it—then forget it. Unfortunately, this attitude has also crept in to our prayers. If God doesn't answer our prayers right away, then we are tempted to quit and maybe even blame God for not coming through. But perseverance in prayer is a necessity, and in this chapter we'll look at why. Why does it sometimes take so long to see an answer to prayer? Is it waiting just for waiting's sake, or could there be a reason beyond that?

Lessons from Three Men and a Frog
(pages 207-209)

Dutch begins this chapter with a poem about two frogs that have fallen into a jar of cream. One accepts his plight as unchangeable and hopelessly lets himself sink to the bottom. The other decides to swim around a little, to put up some resistance at least. His swimming churns the cream to butter, and he is able to hop out unharmed.

1. When have you been like that first frog? What happened?

_____

_____

_____

2. When have you been like that second frog? What happened?

_____

_____

_____

3. Why do you think that perseverance is so difficult for our culture?

_____

_____

_____

4. Read 2 Samuel 23:8-12, which describes three of David's mighty men, all of whom demonstrated and are remembered for tenacity. Describe what each of the following men did and how it shows perseverance.

Josheb-basshebeth (also called Adino)

_____

_____

_____

Eleazar

_____

_____

_____

Shammah

_____

_____

_____

Though perseverance is not listed as one of the Ten Commandments, we are instructed over and over again to possess the same kind of tenacity that David's mighty men had. We probably won't face 800 enemy soldiers at once, nor will we be called upon to defend a plot of lentils, but every day our commitment to godly obedience is tested and we are faced with the choice to dig in our heels or to give up.

Consider the African cheetah, which can run at a speed of 70 miles per hour. It hunts its prey with a definite speed advantage. Yet this incredibly fast cat has a very small heart, causing it to run out of steam quickly. Either it catches its meal fast or it has to give up the chase. Too often we are like that—especially when it comes to prayer. We begin with incredible strength, but we lack the stamina to carry on. If things don't happen fast, we quit. We must increase our staying power. But from where does the ability to persevere come? Is it just a matter of self-determination?

5. Read Galatians 5:22-23. List the nine fruit of the Spirit and circle the word "patience."

The word "patience" in this verse comes from the Greek word *makrothumia* and is translated in the *King James Version* as "longsuffering."[1] As the Holy Spirit continues to work in our lives, He wants to give us the power to be tenacious, to not give up—or, in our common vernacular, to "hang in there, baby!" He is the source of patience; He gives us our ability to be long-suffering.

6. In which area of life is it most difficult for you to show patience?

7. How do we become more patient?

8. Do you agree that believers are sometimes like the African cheetah, beginning well but giving up quickly? Give an example of this from your own experience, especially in regard to prayer.

_____

_____

_____

9. How has a lack of patient endurance affected the Church in general?

_____

_____

_____

Easy Doesn't Do It in Prayer
(pages 209-211)

The majority of the Bible's examples of prayer center on the need for perseverance. Even Jesus, the sinless Son of God, spent many nights in fervent prayer in order to do the work He had come to do. It wasn't automatic. It wasn't easy.

10. Write out Hebrews 5:7.

_____

_____

_____

This describes Jesus' prayer life while He lived on the earth. His prayers weren't quick requests or one-line appeals. He spent hours in the presence of the Father, weeping and crying out to Him. And this same tenacious endurance is the key to victory in prayer. But *why*? Why is persistence required in prayer? Think about how you would answer the following questions about this subject:

- Does God have a certain amount of prayers required for certain situations?
- Do we talk God into things?

- Does God ever "finally decide" to do something?
- Do we earn answers through hard work or perseverance?

Dutch asserts that the answer to all these questions is no. But then why do we need to continue to pray for things? Why can't we just pray once and then wait? Let's take a look at what the Bible has to say.

11. Read Luke 11:1-13. Why did the man get the loaves of bread?

_____

_____

_____

What do you think this passage is saying about persistent prayer?

_____

_____

Persistence is sometimes linked in our minds to wearing someone down until we get what we want. And this is often the idea people take from Jesus' illustration of the man asking for bread. We assume that if we bug God enough, we'll wear Him down and get what we want.

12. Describe a time when you approached God with this attitude. What happened?

_____

_____

_____

13. Do you support the idea that through persistent prayer we are *convincing* God to do something? Why or why not?

_____

_____

_____

14. Why do you think we need to persevere in prayer?

_____

_____

_____

We don't persist in prayer against God. It's about us praying until He decides to give us what we are asking for. The word "persistence" in verse 8 comes from the Greek word *anaideia*, which means "bold unashamedness."[2] It is similar to what we read in Hebrews 4:16, in which we are told to go to God's throne boldly. The idea behind both verses is this: We are free to go before the Father, without shame or a feeling of unworthiness, to ask for His grace to help us. Persistent prayer begins with our understanding that the door is open. We can go to God fearlessly. Persistence is not about repetition as much as it is about access.

15. How would you describe your prayer life in regard to persistence?

_____

_____

_____

16. How does your church encourage persistent prayer?

_____

_____

_____

17. Do you feel the freedom to go boldly before God? Why or why not?

_____

_____

_____

18. When have you allowed a sense of unworthiness or shame keep you from going to God? What did you do about it?

_____

_____

_____

His Throne in Our Hearts
(pages 211-218)

If perseverance in prayer isn't about convincing God, then why do we have to pray repeatedly? Though no one can give a conclusive answer, one idea is that of the substance of prayer. Dutch explains, "Our prayers do more than just motivate the Father to action. They actually release the power of the Holy Spirit from us to accomplish things" (p. 211). Persistent prayer allows a buildup of spiritual power that results in answered prayer. The more we pray, the more "substance" is released.

How does this release occur? Through travail (see Romans 8:26). Through praying in the Spirit (see Ephesians 6:18). Through declaring the Word (see Ephesians 6:17). Through the laying on of hands (see Mark 16:18). And through other forms of God-inspired, Spirit-guided prayer. The bottom line is this: We can know for certain that literal power from the Holy Spirit is released through us as we pray.

As we saw in the last chapter, we are God's temple here on Earth. We are carriers of His presence here and now. So when His power is released, it does not always fall from the sky, but it always comes from *inside of us* as we spend time in His presence in prayer.

19. Dutch explains, "The power of God that brings life, healing and wholeness to the earth flows out from us—the Church" (p. 212). Do you agree? Why or why not?

How have you experienced this?

20. Read John 7:38 and Revelation 22:1-2. In both passages, what is flowing? What results?

_____

_____

_____

The phrases "rivers of living water" and "river of the water of life" are the same in the Greek. What does this infer about the life of God in us and the life of God flowing from the Lamb?

_____

_____

_____

How does this support the idea that God's power is released out of His Church through prayer?

_____

_____

_____

21. Read John 7:39. What did Jesus say was the living water that would flow from within believers?

_____

_____

_____

From these passages we can conclude that God's life, the literal power and energy of God, flows out of us. He lives in us to enable us to represent Him to the world. And this power is measurable; it has substance.

22. Explain in your own words why we must persevere in prayer.

_____

_____

_____

Releasing the River of Power
(pages 218-221)

Prayer is more than just asking God to do something. It is a matter of releasing enough power in the Spirit to get the job done. In other words, rather than us waiting on God, perhaps He is waiting on us to pray and pray again until there is enough power to accomplish the task, to release the answer.

Before you get the idea that we are somehow conjuring up power and playing the role of God, let me reiterate that the power is His—His *alone*. But we, as His dwelling place, can release spiritual power as we offer Spirit-filled prayer. Consider the examples of Elijah and Daniel.

23. Read 1 Kings 17:17-24. What had happened to the widow's son?

_____

_____

_____

How many times did Elijah cover the boy and pray?

_____

_____

What resulted from Elijah's prayers?

_____

_____

24. Read 1 Kings 18:1,41-44. What did God say He would send on the land?

_____

_____

_____

How many times did Elijah pray? In what posture?

_____

_____

_____

What resulted from his repeated prayers?

_____

_____

_____

25. Read Daniel 10:12-14. When did God send Daniel's answer?

_____

_____

_____

How long did it take to get the answer?

_____

_____

_____

What had hindered it?

_____

_____

_____

26. How do these examples support the idea that prayer is more than just asking God for something, that it is releasing power in the Spirit until there is enough to accomplish the task?

_____

_____

_____

_____

Do you agree with this idea? Why or why not?

_____

_____

_____

Dutch explains, "I am not limiting God's power. I am fully aware that one word from God could rout every demon in hell. What must be factored in is God's decision to work on the earth through man. It seems reasonable to me that if a man's prayers were responsible for the angel being dispatched, they would also be the key to breaking through with the message" (p. 218).

27. How does understanding this give you a new outlook on persevering prayer?

_____

_____

_____

28. Explain why we need to continue to pray about something until the answer comes.

_____

_____

_____

29. When have you repeatedly prayed for something? What kept you persevering? What resulted?

_____

_____

_____

We must not assume that persevering in prayer means vain repetition. In fact, Jesus condemns this. Rather, we persevere through Spirit-led prayer to see spiritual power released so that He can move in a given situation to bring life and healing, to restore liberty and freedom. When spiritual power doesn't seem to be released, the problem is not the source of the power. The problem is the conduit—us. Like African cheetahs, we give up because we lack stamina—spiritual stamina, in our case. Irregular and casual praying won't accomplish the miraculous. God asks us to become radical intercessors—not weird or mystical, but determined and persistent. We must engage in committed, determined, systematic prayer to see the power of God released in dynamic, supernatural ways.

30. Write out James 5:16.

_____

_____

_____

How is the prayer of a righteous man described in this verse? What can it accomplish?

_____

_____

_____

The Amplified Bible expounds James 5:16 to read, "The earnest (heartfelt, continued) prayer of a righteous man makes tremendous power available [dynamic in its working]."

31. How does this description compare with your prayer life?

_____

_____

_____

How would you describe your prayer life?

_____

_____

_____

32. Does the information in this chapter stir you to persistent prayer? What will you do about it?

_____

_____

_____

The same power that raised Jesus from the dead lives in us, if we are His followers. The same power that created the world dwells in those who belong to Him. The same power that defeated darkness and broke the stronghold of sin and death is at work inside us. Through prayer—

consistent and long-suffering prayer—we can see that power released to accomplish God's will and establish His kingdom.

Tipping the Prayer Bowls of Heaven
(pages 221-226)

How do we know that our persistent prayers have real substance that can effect change in the world around us? Because the Bible tells us that our prayers accumulate and are placed in bowls for use at specific times decreed by God. Whether literal or not, God says that He keeps our prayers for use at the proper time.

33. Read Revelation 5:8. With what are the golden bowls of incense filled?

34. Read Revelation 8:3-5. What did the angel do with the prayers of the saints? What resulted on Earth?

35. What does this say about the accumulation of prayer? How does this connect with our understanding of the need for persistence in prayer until we see the answer?

36. Write out Ephesians 3:20-21. Underline the phrases "to Him who is able" and "according to the power."

When we intercede, cooperating with the Spirit of God, it releases Him to go out from us and hover over a situation to release His life-birthing energy until that which we are asking for comes forth. We can re-present Him on Earth through dedicated and obedient intercession.

One final thought. What happens when you are persistent but do not see the answer you were expecting? Should you give up? No! The truths contained in the Bible are all we need to know at this point, but they are certainly not all there is to know. Though now we see as through a dim glass, one day it will be replaced by 20/20 vision (see 1 Corinthians 13:12). But our lack of understanding should never be the reason we stop doing what the Word says. In the face of discouragement or disappointment, we must continue to pray, continue to believe and never ever give up. Release His power, believe for His purposes to be accomplished, and daily lend your heart to fervent intercession. God is at work.

37. For what situations is God calling you to begin persistent prayer? List them below as a point of commitment. Then take a few moments and begin to release spiritual power through prayer. Ask for the Holy Spirit to hover over these situations to bring new life. Tear down the strongholds that have restricted God's fullness. Speak His Word over these areas. Thank the Lord that He is at work, taking the substance of your prayers and pouring them out in blessing and release.

Notes
 1. James Strong, *The New Strong's Exhaustive Concordance of the Bible* (Nashville, TN: Thomas Nelson Publishers, 1984), ref. no. 3115.
 2. Jack W. Hayford, *Prayer Is Invading the Impossible* (South Plainfield, NJ: Logos International, 1977), p. 55.

CHAPTER THIRTEEN

ACTIONS THAT SPEAK AND WORDS THAT PERFORM

Lie on your left side for over a year, and then lie on your right side for 40 days. Cook your meal over cow manure. Shave your head and weigh your hair on a scale. Hide a torch inside a clay pot. Marry a prostitute. Tie two sticks together. Name your child Lo-Ammi. March around a city. Break perfume over someone's feet. Turn your face away from a nation.

What do all these things have in common? They are all biblical examples of obedience. What?! How can this be? Does this mean that *we* have to do these things? Read on!

The Boomerang Anointing: Action and Declaration
(pages 230-232)

Dutch makes the statement: "There is an interesting aspect of intercession few people understand and still fewer do. It is *prophetic action and declaration*" (p. 231). And that's what this chapter will center on: those times when God directs specific actions or declarations that declare His greater purpose for an area, nation or people. Actions that, like prayer, bring forth a spiritual release of power.

1. What do you understand the word "prophetic" to mean?

_____

_____

_____

2. How can an action be prophetic?

_____

_____

_____

Something that is prophetic can either be foretelling or forthtelling. This means that prophetic words and actions, under the specific guidance of the Holy Spirit, can either refer to future things (foretelling) or declare something that God is saying here and now (forthtelling). Both of these aspects of the prophetic release the glory of God and prepare the way for His ministry. This is not to say that God needs to be released because He is in any way bound; He is not. It simply means that Spirit-prompted prophetic actions and declarations are part of the way God may choose to move in a given situation. As we are obedient to His instructions, we release His creative and effectual Word upon the earth, and things change.

3. What is the difference between foretelling and forthtelling as it relates to prophetic prayer?

_____

_____

_____

4. Dutch purports, "Obedience to God brings a response from God" (p. 231). Do you agree? Why or why not? Try to find a scriptural basis for your answer.

_____

_____

_____

How does this statement connect with prophetic actions and declarations?

_____

_____

_____

5. In your understanding, how can an action or declaration lead to spiritual release?

_____

_____

_____

6. Have you ever been prompted by the Holy Spirit to do a specific action or make a declaration that released spiritual power? What happened?

_____

_____

_____

Dutch gives a complete definition of this concept by stating, "Prophetic action or declaration is something said or done in the natural realm at the direction of God that prepares the way for Him to move in the spiritual realm, which then consequently effects change in the natural realm" (p. 232). In other words, when we do what God says, our words and actions impact the heavens, which in turn impact the earth. Boomerang!

Let's consider action and declaration individually, delving into the Word to see what God has to say about these unique methods of intercession.

Prophetic Action
(pages 232-236)

A prophetic action is a _God-inspired action that releases spiritual power to bring about His will_. Moses, Naaman and a blind man are three biblical people who were instructed to perform a prophetic act.

7. Read Exodus 14:13-22. In verse 16, what did God instruct Moses to do?

_____

_____

_____

_____

What happened as a result?

_____

_____

_____

Do you think the same result would have been accomplished if Moses had not done as God instructed? Why or why not?

_____

_____

_____

_____

8. Read Exodus 17:3-6. What were God's instructions to Moses?

_____

_____

_____

What would have happened if Moses hadn't followed through as God commanded?

_____

_____

_____

9. Read Exodus 17:8-13. According to verse 9, what did Moses hold in his hands?

_____

_____

_____

When his hands were lifted, what happened? When they fell, what happened?

_____

_____

_____

_____

Would the Israelites have enjoyed victory if Moses had given up due to weariness?

_____

_____

_____

How did this prophetic spiritual act impact the natural realm?

_____

_____

_____

10. In the above three passages, what was Moses holding? Why do you think this was important?

_____

_____

_____

11. Read 2 Kings 13:14-19. According to verses 15-17, what did Elisha ask King Joash to do and what declaration did Elisha make?

_____

_____

_____

According to verses 18-19, what did Elisha ask King Joash to do and what declaration did Elisha make?

_____

_____

_____

According to verse 19, what would have happened if the king had hit the ground more than three times?

_____

_____

_____

12. Read 2 Kings 5:1,9-14. What illness was plaguing Naaman?

_____

_____

_____

What did Elisha tell him to do?

_____

_____

What was Naaman's attitude about these instructions?

_____

_____

_____

How did Naaman end up responding and what was the result?

_____

_____

_____

What do you think would have happened if Naaman had refused to do as Elisha said?

_____

_____

_____

13. Read John 9:6-7. How did Jesus heal the blind man?

_____

_____

_____

Why would He choose to heal him this way?

_____

_____

_____

How could this be described as a prophetic act?

_____

_____

_____

A wooden staff that parts seas and brings water from rocks, raised hands that strengthen an army victory, arrows that ensure an enemy's defeat, a river that cures leprosy, mud that makes blind men see—let's face it, prophetic acts can seem a bit eccentric. But looking over these passages, we must understand that it is not the action in and of itself that brings the answer or the victory; rather, it is the humble obedience to follow God's instructions that releases spiritual power. When we cry out to Him in prayer and He leads us to do prophetic actions, we must obey. These actions are preparing the way for answers to prayer.

14. What's the most unusual prophetic act you've seen someone do? What resulted?

_____

_____

_____

15. How can you tell whether or not an action is truly prophetic and not just a weird idea?

_____

_____

_____

16. Describe a time when you have seen someone act on what he or she felt was God's instructions, only to find that his or her actions did not bring about a release of God's power. How has this shaded your belief in God's ability to inspire people to prophetic action?

_____

_____

_____

_____

17. Do you think God still uses prophetic actions to prepare the way for answers to prayer? How have you experienced this personally?

_____

_____

_____

18. What place should prophetic actions have in the Church today?

_____

_____

_____

Prophetic Declaration
(pages 236-239)

Not only does God inspire people to perform actions that are prophetic, but He also impresses people to make bold declarations about what He intends to do in a given situation. These prophetic declarations are *powerful releases of His Word that bring about changes in the heavenlies and on the earth*. Spoken not to the people present at the time but to the spiritual realm at large, prophetic declarations release spiritual power so that God's revealed purpose can be accomplished. Jeremiah, Micah, Hosea, Ezekiel and Isaiah are just some of the people through whom God spoke prophetically, as recorded in the Bible.

19. Read Jeremiah 6:18-19; 22:29 and Micah 1:2. To whom are Jeremiah and Micah told to speak? Is this naturally possible?

_____

_____

Why would God inspire them to speak this way?

_____

_____

20. Read Hosea 6:5. Through what was the judgment of God released?

_____

_____

_____

21. Read Ezekiel 37:1-14. What specific prophetic declarations did God tell Ezekiel to make? What happened as a result of each declaration?

_____

_____

_____

How did Ezekiel's words prepare the way for God's power to be released?

_____

_____

_____

22. Read Isaiah 55:11. What did God mean when He said "My word . . . shall not return to Me empty"?

_____

_____

_____

_____

Who had spoken His Word in this book of the Bible?

_____

_____

_____

How does God speak His Word today?

_____

_____

_____

_____

23. How would you answer someone who claims that in our day and age God does not speak directly to people?

_____

_____

_____

24. What standards can you use to measure whether or not a prophetic declaration is really inspired from God?

_____

_____

_____

Saying What God Says
(pages 239-245)

The New Testament word for "confession" is *homologia* and means "say the same thing."[1] Prophetic declaration is just that: saying the same thing that God is saying. It is us echoing aloud the message He has already spoken. Prophetic declarations are instances when we are inspired by God to speak His Word into a situation to release spiritual power. It is important to realize that it is not our words but His Word that makes the difference.

The Word of God is called a "seed" in the Scriptures (see Luke 8:11 and 1 Peter 1:23). Several of the Greek words for "seed" are *spora, sporos* and *sperma*, all of which come from the same root word, *speiro*.[2] It's easy to see that we get our English words "spore" and "sperm" from them. The significance is that God's Word is a seed that reproduces life.

25. Read the following Scriptures and write down how the Word affects our lives:

Psalm 107:20

_____

_____

_____

Matthew 13:23

_____

_____

John 8:31-32

_____

_____

John 15:3

_____

_____

_____

1 Peter 1:23

_____

_____

_____

These are just a few verses about God's Word, but the power of the Word is clearly seen. It heals, cleanses and frees us. When we speak that same Word under the guidance of the Holy Spirit, it will do the same. And that is what prophetic declaration is all about.

26. Read Job 22:26-30. Write out verse 28 and underline the word "decree."

_____

_____

In this verse, God says that when we decree or declare a word, He will establish it for us. What amazing horizons are opened for the intercessor who is surrendered to the leadership of the Holy Spirit! As He leads us to speak a word, we can know it will be accomplished! As we sow the seed of the Word through bold, prophetic declaration and then tend to that seed with persistent prayer, it will produce a harvest. God _will_ move!

27. Write out Ephesians 3:10.

_____

_____

_____

How is the wisdom of God to be made known?

_____

_____

_____

What does this have to do with prophetic declaration?

_____

_____

_____

28. Dutch gives three modern-day examples of prophetic action and declaration. Read each one and explain how you see prophetic action and prophetic declaration at work.

Dick Eastman, president of Every Home for Christ, felt led by God to go to Germany. He understood that God wanted him to place his hands on the Berlin Wall (which had not yet fallen) and declare "In Jesus' Name, come down."

_____

_____

_____

A group of young people marched behind Norm Stone, a man who had been led by God to walk across the United States seven times as an act of repentance and intercession for the babies murdered through abortion. These young people symbolized a new generation that would not be lost through Satan's schemes and devices.

_____

_____

_____

Dutch participated in a three-day read-a-thon, reading the entire Bible aloud in front of the Capitol in Washington, D.C. What would be the purpose of just reading the Bible aloud with no explanation, no sermons and no exposition?

When God's Word is declared in faith, through Spirit-inspired confession, it seeds God's will into the earth and causes it to be established. Things change. Circumstances come into right order. Why? Because His Word never returns void; it always accomplishes what He sends it forth to do. As intercessors, we can play a part in seeing His Word released. When He inspires us to perform actions or make declarations that foretell or forthtell His plans, let's do it without fear or intimidation. Let's be bold and sprinkle the seeds of His Word over the situations we or those we pray for face. As we obey the Lord in prophetic action and declaration, things will change!

29. How has your idea of prophetic actions and declarations changed?

---

30. Do you sense God's wanting to move in your prayer life in this way? How?

Notes

1. Spiros Zodhiates, *Hebrew-Greek Key Study Bible—New American Standard*, rev. ed. (Chattanooga, TN: AMG Publishers, 1990), p. 1861.
2. James Strong, *The New Strong's Exhaustive Concordance of the Bible* (Nashville, TN: Thomas Nelson Publishers, 1984), ref. nos. 4687, 4690, 4701, 4703.

CHAPTER FOURTEEN

THE WATCHMAN ANOINTING

We began this study by asking a lot of questions. At this point you should have a lot of answers, too! (You may want to go back and review some of those questions, seeing how you would now respond to them.) Let's recap some of the main ideas about intercession that have been presented:

- God chose from the beginning of creation to work on Earth through humans, not independently of them. Intercession can be summarized as mediating between two parties and pleading for or representing one party to another.
- Intercessors meet (*paga*) with God; they also meet with powers of darkness.
- We can establish spiritual boundaries—No Trespassing signs— that disallow enemy access.
- We can demolish the strongholds of the enemy and bring every high thing captive.
- Through prayer we can bear another's burden, taking it away.
- In prayer we can release spiritual power that births new life.
- We can speak His powerful, creative Word and direct His light into dark situations.
- Prophetic action and declaration are acts of obedience to God that bring a response from Him.

As we draw this study to a close, the last aspect of intercession we will focus on is the watchman anointing.

Be on the Alert
(pages 250-254)

Over and over again the Bible adjures us to watchfulness. We are to remain on the lookout! Nowhere is this a more vital request than in intercessory prayer. Intercessors are mandated to keep their eyes on the horizon in order to pray against Satan's schemes.

1. Write out Ephesians 6:18 and underline the phrase "be on the alert."

   _____

   _____

   _____

2. Write out 1 Peter 5:8 and underline the phrase "be on the alert."

   _____

   _____

   _____

3. Write out 2 Corinthians 2:11 and underline the phrase "not ignorant."

   _____

   _____

   _____

Each of these verses mentions our enemy and commands us to be alert, or watchful, both for ourselves and for those we pray for.

4. Describe a time when someone's watchfulness prevented trouble in your life.

   _____

   _____

   _____

5. Describe a time when your watchfulness prevented trouble for someone else.

_____
_____
_____

6. How does watchfulness relate to intercessory prayer?

_____
_____
_____

7. Is it really possible to see Satan's schemes and then to prevent them? Explain your response.

_____
_____
_____

8. Dutch reaches four conclusions based on the preceding verses. Read each statement and comment on whether or not you agree and why.

Protection from the attacks of our enemy—even for believers—is not automatic.

_____
_____
_____

God's plan is to warn or alert us to Satan's tactics.

_____
_____

We must be alert—remain watchful—or we won't pick up on God's attempts to warn us of Satan's attacks and plans.

_____
_____
_____

If we are not alert and watchful, if we are ignorant of Satan's schemes, he will take the bigger portion.

_____

_____

_____

Scripture makes it clear that we have a part to play in warding off the attack of the enemy. If God commands us to be alert, it must be because He is willing to warn us. Though He is sovereign, He has chosen to include humanity in the extension of His will on this earth. Because of this, we must take up our role and re-present Him rightly. But God doesn't leave us to fend for ourselves; instead, He comes alongside us to guide and instruct, to warn and preserve. Intercessors are the watchmen who keep their eyes on the horizon and who are attentive to God's leading.

Two New Testament words that convey the idea of watching are *gregoreuo* and *agrupneo*. Both essentially mean to stay awake. Read the following Scriptures, all of which contain one of these words: Mark 14:34,38; Luke 21:36; 1 Corinthians 16:13; Colossians 4:2; and 1 Peter 5:8.

9. Have you or someone you know ever served as a watchman, maybe in the military or in a career context? Describe the duties associated with that position.

_____

_____

_____

10. Draw some parallels between being a watchman in the natural realm and being a watchman in the spiritual realm. How are they the same? How are they different?

_____

_____

_____

11. Are all Christians called to be spiritual watchmen? Why or why not?

_____

_____

_____

Biblical Watchmen
(pages 254-259)

The term "watchman" comes from the Old Testament. Today we would use the words "sentry," "patrol," "guard" or "lookout." The watchmen were responsible for protecting primarily two things: fields from thieves and animals, and cities from invading forces. Watchmen were stationed on rocks, lookout towers or city walls in order to have a better view of what was coming. Sometimes the guard was maintained 24 hours a day—especially during harvest time, when the potential for loss was greater. Read the following passages, which describe where watchmen were stationed and what they were to look for: Isaiah 21:6-8; 62:6; and Jeremiah 51:12.

The watchmen looked for two things: messengers and enemies. Skilled watchmen even came to recognize far-off messengers by their running stride (see 2 Samuel 18:27). God wants us, intercessors for the Body of Christ, to develop this type of sensitivity. We should be able to recognize "messengers" and messages that are good as well as those that are harmful before they arrive at the gates of the Church. Dutch asserts, "Most false doctrine, division and general destruction in the Body of Christ could be averted if the watchmen would watch and the leaders would listen!" (p. 256).

12. Read Acts 20:28-31. What was Paul's admonition to the elders of the Ephesian church?

_____

_____

_____

13. Read 2 Peter 2:1-2. What is Peter's warning to the churches?

_____

_____

14. How does intercessory prayer play a part in keeping false teachers out of the Church?

_____

_____

_____

15. How can you distinguish between a true warning from God and a personal apprehension?

_____

_____

_____

16. Have you ever felt uneasy about a situation or teaching, only to find out that your uneasiness was a warning meant to alert others to danger? What happened?

_____

_____

_____

17. How can the Body of Christ better benefit from the watchmen's warnings?

_____

_____

_____

The watchmen also looked for enemies. When they saw potential danger, they sounded a horn to alert people to action. As intercessors, we are called to alert the Body to the attacks of Satan so that it can defend itself.

18. How have you seen the Body of Christ preserved from an attack of Satan through intercessory prayer?

_____

_____

_____

19. How have you seen the lack of warning allow the devil to gain ground against the Church and hinder the advance of the kingdom of God?

_____

_____

_____

Unfortunately, many believers choose to ignore Satan altogether. Yet the Bible makes it clear that we have an enemy and that ignoring him will not make him go away. Watchmen see his attack and alert the Body to the need for warfare.

20. How have you seen imbalance, by either ignoring Satan altogether or looking for demons behind every door?

_____

_____

_____

21. How can believers achieve biblical balance?

_____

_____

_____

Dutch explains, "Be infatuated with and in awe of Jesus—be aware of the enemy. Love worship, not warfare, but when necessary, go to war" (p. 258). What an apt and fitting way to describe how intercessors should approach being watchmen. We love Jesus and focus our eyes on Him. But when He alerts us, by His Spirit, to danger, we take up our swords and fight.

Be Defensive—Keep the Serpent Out!
(pages 260-265)

In addition to guarding fields and cities, watchmen also created a hedge around whatever they were protecting. The Hebrew words for "watchman" are _natsar, shamar_ and _tsaphah_. They mean to guard or protect something not only by watching over it but also by "hedging around" it, as with thorns.[1] In fact, the word *tsaphah* can mean "lean forward and peer into the distance."[2]

22. Read Genesis 2:15 and notice the word "keep." What was Adam charged to keep, take care of or guard?

_____

_____

_____

From what do you think Adam was protecting it?

_____

_____

_____

23. Read Genesis 3:24 and notice the word "guard." What was the cherubim guarding?

_____

_____

_____

From whom was he guarding it?

_____

_____

24. Read Genesis 30:31 and notice the word "keep." What was Jacob protecting?

_____

_____

_____

25. Read 1 Samuel 26:15; 28:2; and notice the words "guarded" and "bodyguard." What were they to guard?

_____

_____

_____

26. Read Proverbs 4:23 and notice the word "watch." Over what are we to keep vigilant guard?

_____

_____

_____

27. The three Hebrew words for "watchman" are also translated in the following ways. Consider each one and write a quick explanation of how it might pertain to intercessory prayer.

Keep or keeper

_____

_____

Guard

_____

_____

Bodyguard

_____

Doorkeeper

_____

_____

Gatekeeper

_____

_____

Preserve or preserver

_____

_____

Pay attention

_____

_____

Observe

_____

_____

Behold

_____

_____

Beware

_____

_____

Protect

_____

_____

Maintain

_____

_____

28. How does the above list broaden your understanding of what it means to be a watchman in prayer?

_____

_____

_____

29. What message was God giving to all believers when He placed Adam in the Garden and told him to tend it?

_____

_____

30. Are there areas in your own life where the serpent has been let into the Garden? How can prayer reestablish the border?

_____

_____

31. Are there areas in which our country has let in the serpent? How can prayer reestablish spiritual boundaries?

_____

_____

_____

Dutch explains, "God is raising up prophetic intercessors—watchmen—*to keep the serpent out!* Men and women who will 'lean forward, peering into the distance' watching for the enemy's attacks. Sentries, bodyguards, gatekeepers, boundary setters and preservers in His kingdom" (p. 265).

32. How do you see God calling you to be a watchman? What are you going to do about it?

_____

_____

_____

Be Offensive—Lay Siege!
(pages 265-274)

There is another aspect of watchman prayer that needs to be addressed: the idea of offensive warfare. In the following verses, the words for "watchman" have meanings similar to "lay siege," "lie in wait to ambush" or "spy upon." Please look up each verse and note how the Hebrew word is translated.

- "spies" in Judges 1:24
- "kept watch" ("under seige," *NIV*) in 2 Samuel 11:16
- "beseiged" in Isaiah 1:8
- "besiegers" and "watchmen" in Jeremiah 4:16-17
- "place men in ambush" in Jeremiah 51:12

From these verses we can understand that not only are we to defend, but we are also to take a proactive stance to reclaim ground the enemy has taken. We can lay spiritual siege to any place the devil has captured and, by the power of the Holy Spirit and persistent prayer, take it back for the Kingdom. Where our ignorance has allowed Satan's plans to prosper, we can go to God and receive instructions about how to cut off Satan's supply lines and disable his power to rule.

As an example of this, Dutch tells how two women laid siege to their neighborhood by walking and praying over each home systematically for a season of prayer. Soon they heard reports of how their neighbors had come to Christ and accepted His gift of salvation. This is offensive watchman prayer. This is our privilege as intercessors.

33. How have you personally seen this type of strategic, offensive prayer put into practice? What resulted?

---

34. In what ways can prayer "cut off the supply lines" of the enemy?

---

35. How may other aspects of intercession (e.g., the lightning of God, boundary setting, prophetic actions and words) have a part in proactive intercessory prayer such as this?

This type of watchman prayer can benefit not only individuals but also entire nations and people groups. There is a biblical precedent for God's dealing with whole nations. Abraham interceded for a city (see Genesis 18:22-33) and Moses for a nation (see Exodus 32:9-14). Consider how the prophets addressed "all Israel" or other nations, how entire cities were judged or released, how whole people groups—such as the Hebrews—had a special calling and purpose, and how people groups experienced corporate righteousness or corporate sin.

36. Along these lines, write out 2 Chronicles 7:14.

_____

_____

_____

_____

What can our prayers bring? Who is affected?

_____

_____

_____

_____

The city of Resistencia, Argentina, was impacted by systematic, offensive intercession and warfare. The Church in Resistencia prayed against the powers of darkness over the city until they were confident that there had been spiritual breakthrough. Then they embarked upon full-scale evangelism, taking the message of the gospel to everyone they could. The city was revolutionized and a large number of people were saved.

37. Do you think it is possible for nations to experience revival, or is it strictly on an individual basis? Why?

_____

_____

_____

38. How have you seen intercession reach a group of people?

_____

_____

_____

39. What will it take to see our nation experience revival?

_____

_____

_____

To close the book, Dutch challenges, "Are you ready to walk in your calling as an intercessor? . . . To re-present Jesus as the reconciler and the warrior? . . . To distribute His benefits and victory? . . . To meet, to carry away, to set boundaries? Are you ready to birth, to liberate, to strike the mark? . . . To fill some bowls, to make some declarations, to watch and pray? Are you ready?" (pp. 273-274).

40. What is your response to Dutch's challenge? Are you ready?

Notes

1. James Strong, *The New Strong's Exhaustive Concordance of the Bible* (Nashville, TN: Thomas Nelson Publishers, 1990), ref. no. 8104.
2. Ibid., ref. no. 6822.

DISCUSSION LEADER'S GUIDE

The purpose of *Intercessory Prayer* and the *Intercessory Prayer Study Guide* is to ignite and empower the prayer life of those who read and study them. As the group grows in faith and unity, you may want to implement some of the prayer tactics mentioned in *Intercessory Prayer*, such as using prayer cloths, prayer-walking and engaging in spiritual warfare for each other.

As a leader it is important to be sensitive to the maturity level of the group. It is also important that you do not impose your beliefs on those who differ in the way they worship the Lord.

The optimum-sized discussion group is 10 to 15 people. A smaller group can make continuity a problem when too few members attend. A larger group will require strong leadership skills to create a sense of belonging and meaningful participation for each person.

If you are leading a group that already meets regularly, such as a Sunday School class or weekly home group, decide how many weeks to spend on the series. Be sure to plan for any holidays that may occur during your scheduled meetings.

Use creativity. The 14 chapters of the study guide can be tailored to fit your group's time commitment—anywhere from 7 to 14 weeks. If you cover more than one chapter each week, you will be able to adjust the duration of your group study meeting and also provide time for personal sharing.

The first session would provide a perfect time for an open forum to create a sense of unity as you begin the series. A time for introduction followed by nonthreatening questions is often helpful for building close ties within the group. Chapter 1 can be used as the introduction. Consider one or more of the following questions:

1. Are you satisfied with your prayer life? If not, where are you struggling?

2. Why do you think prayer is such a lacking discipline in the Body of Christ?

3. What do you hope to gain from studying this book?

4. After reading chapter 1, do you think we should pray only once or do you think we need to be persistent? Why?

5. If you could ask God one question about prayer, what would it be?

Such questions will create a sense of identity among the class members and help them to discover their similarities.

Many individual questions may arise that will significantly contribute to the group's understanding of the subject. Group members should be encouraged to maintain lists of their questions. Suggest that they be submitted anonymously and combine them together to eliminate repetition. Many questions may be answered by the time the series reaches its conclusion. It is, therefore, a good idea to wait until your last session to discuss them.

Enlist a co-leader to assist with calling class members to remind them of meeting dates, times and places. Your co-leader can also make arrangements for refreshments and child care.

People will have a greater appreciation for their books if they are responsible for paying for them. They will also be more apt to finish the course if they have invested in their own materials.

Be sure to have several extra Bibles available. *The Living Bible* is often helpful for people who have little or no Bible background; however, it is important to explain that the *New American Standard Bible* differs considerably and will be the main version used in this book.

Be aware of these basic guidelines to aid group dynamics:

1. Arrange seating in a semicircle with the leader included rather than standing in front. This setting invites participation.

2. Create a discussion-friendly atmosphere. The following tips are helpful for guiding discussions:

a. Receive statements from group members without being judgmental, even if you disagree with them. If they are clearly unbiblical or unfair, you can ask questions that clarify the issue; but outright rejection of comments will stifle open participation.

b. If a question or comment deviates from the subject, either suggest that it be dealt with at another time or ask the group if they want to pursue the new issue now.

c. If one person monopolizes the discussion, direct a few questions specifically to someone else. Or tactfully interrupt the dominator by saying, "Excuse me, that's a good thought, and I wonder what the rest of us think about that." Talk with the person privately and enlist that person's help in drawing others into the discussion.

d. Make it easy and comfortable for everyone to share or ask questions, but don't insist that anyone do so. Reluctant participants can warm to the idea of sharing by being asked to read a passage from the book. Pair a shy person with someone else for a discussion apart from the main group, and ask reluctant participants to write down a comment to be shared with the larger group.

e. If someone asks you a question and you don't know the answer, admit it and move on. If the question calls for insight from personal experience, invite others to comment on it; however, be careful that this sharing is limited. If it requires special knowledge, offer to look for an answer in the library or from a theologian or minister, and report your findings later.

3. Guard against rescuing. The purpose of this group is to learn to pray for others, not fix them. This doesn't mean that poignant moments won't come up or unhappy problems won't be shared, but the group is for sharing and prayer—not fixing others. The leader should be open and honest about wanting to grow with the group instead of coming across as an authority on the subject.

4. Start and stop on time, according to the schedule agreed upon before the series begins. This is especially important for those who have to hire a babysitter or arise early for work the next morning.

5. During each session, lead group members in discussing the questions and exercises at the end of each chapter. If you have more than 8 to 10 class members, consider dividing into small groups, and then invite each group to share one or two insights with the larger group.

6. Be sensitive. Some people may feel comfortable praying for others, but don't force those who don't. It is necessary to set aside a time either at the beginning or end of the meeting to pray for those in need.

7. Encourage members of the group to pray daily for each other. This will perpetuate a sense of unity and love.

8. As a leader, pray regularly for the sessions and the participants, asking the Holy Spirit to hover over each person throughout the week. The Lord will honor your willingness to guide His people toward a more intimate relationship with Him.

Discussion Questions

To facilitate group discussion of the ideas presented in the study guide, you may want to ask the following questions in your group. Be creative:

You may find that including other questions from the study guide or creating your own will better meet your group's needs.

Chapter One

1. Are you satisfied with your prayer life? If not, where are you struggling?
2. Why do you think prayer is such a lacking discipline in the Body of Christ?
3. What do you hope to gain from studying this book?
4. After reading chapter 1, do you think we should pray only once or do you think we need to be persistent? Why?
5. If you could ask God one question about prayer, what would it be?

Chapter Two

1. How complete was Adam's (humankind's) dominion upon the earth? Can you explain how this relates to the necessity of prayer in order for God to work?
2. What did God mean when He said we were made in His image and likeness?
3. How does the story of Elijah praying for rain (see 1 Kings 18) reinforce our assertion that God works through prayer? How about Daniel's prayer for the restoration of Israel?
4. What is the root meaning of "glory"? How does this relate to prayer and representation?
5. How does it feel to be a partner with God?

Chapter Three

1. How are intercession and mediation related?
2. Can you explain what Dutch meant when he said Christ was THE intercessor and that our *prayers* are an extension of His *work*?
3. Explain the two aspects of Christ's intercession—reconciling and separating—relating it to humankind's twofold need created by the Fall.
4. What is the significance of being a "sent one"?

Chapter Four

1. In what way does a meeting picture intercession? How does *paga* establish the correlation between the two?

2. Explain the two opposite kinds of meetings discussed in this chapter. How does each one represent Calvary?
3. Define *luo* and comment on Christ doing it and the Church doing it.
4. Think of someone you know who needs a meeting with God. How and when can you help facilitate this?

Chapter Five
1. Explain the two types of bearing in the Scriptures. How do they pertain to intercession? What does *paga* have to do with bearing?
2. Can you explain how the scapegoat is a picture of intercession?
3. How does the account of Joshua and the Israelites in Joshua 10:22-27 picture the partnership between Christ and the Church?
4. In what way does Psalm 110 picture the relationship between Jesus and the Church?

Chapter Six
1. How is the connection between *paga* and protection made?
2. Is all protection automatic for Christians? Is everything that happens to us allowed by God or do our actions and prayers have a part in it? Explain.
3. Comment on consistency in prayer as it relates to protection.
4. Explain the difference between *chronos* and *kairos* and how this relates to intercession.
5. For whom will you post a No Trespassing sign?

Chapter Seven
1. Can you explain the connection between Genesis 28:10-17 and Romans 8:26-27? Be sure to include comments on *paga*, the butterfly anointing and praying in the Spirit.
2. What does the Holy Spirit do to help us in our weaknesses?
3. Think of situations where you don't know how to pray as you should. Make a decision to allow the Holy Spirit to help you. Decide when you're going to give Him the opportunity to do so.

Chapter Eight

1. How have we defined "travail" improperly and how has this hindered intercession?
2. Explain the connection between Genesis 1:1-2; Deuteronomy 32:10-18; Luke 1:35 and travail.
3. What do we mean when we speak of the "moving" of the Holy Spirit?
4. When and where can one travail? For what can one travail? Can you think of a situation in which God might want to do some birthing through your prayers?

Chapter Nine

1. What are the two opposite activities usually needed in intercession? Why are both necessary? Does the meaning and use of *paga* reinforce this?
2. Explain 2 Corinthians 2:11. How does it reinforce the fact that we're not to ignore Satan?
3. Can you explain the connection among worship, waiting and warfare? How does Joshua picture this? Similarly, what insights can be gleaned from Mary and Martha concerning this?
4. Why would spiritual warfare ever be necessary if Christ defeated and destroyed the powers of darkness? Include comments on the difference between authority and power.

Chapter Ten

1. What is meant by the word "veil" in 2 Corinthians 4:3? How does this apply to unsaved people? Can you explain how this is related to a biblical revelation?
2. What is meant by Satan "blinding" the minds of unbelievers? How is this connected to the fall of humanity? How is this significant where men (versus women) are concerned?
3. Explain the meaning of illumination, or enlightenment. Can you describe the analogy to this and photography?
4. What is the true meaning of repentance? How is this connected to biblical revelation?
5. Define a stronghold. Now describe the three aspects of the stronghold in unbelievers and how intercession can be applied to each.

6. For whom are you going to tear down strongholds?

Chapter Eleven
1. How is *paga* related to lightning?
2. Explain the connection between God's light/lightning and His judgments. Can you explain how this happened at the Cross?
3. What is the relationship between God, light, His sword and our intercession?
4. Where is the holy of holies? How does this relate to intercession?
5. Think of a situation where light overcame darkness. How did God do it? Now, think of a current situation in which intercession can be used to see the same results.

Chapter Twelve
1. What is the real lesson being taught by the story in Luke 11:5-13?
2. What is meant by "the substance" of prayer? How does this relate to perseverance?
3. Can you think of any situations where you may have stopped praying before your "bowl" was filled? Are there any current situations in your life that might need more power released to receive an answer?

Chapter Thirteen
1. Define prophetic action and declaration. Explain how they "release" God. Now give some biblical examples.
2. Can you explain the connection among God's Word, seeds and our Holy Spirit-inspired declarations?
3. Can you find some verses of Scripture that would be good to decree for an individual's salvation? For healing? How about Scriptures to decree over your city?

Chapter Fourteen
1. Can you summarize the four conclusions drawn from Ephesians 6:18, 1 Peter 5:8 and 2 Corinthians 2:11? Using the verses themselves, give reasons for these conclusions.
2. Describe the functions and responsibilities of Old Testament watchmen. How do they symbolize watching intercession?

3. Based on the definitions and usages of the three words for watchman, can you give some summary statements about the defensive aspect of the watchman anointing? How can you apply this to your family? Your pastor? Your church?
4. Describe the offensive aspect of the watchman anointing. Can you relate it to intercession for an individual? How about for a city?
5. Think of ways you and your prayer group can lay siege to your city. Do it!

Your Prayers Are Powerful

DUTCH SHEETS

OVER 500,000 COPIES SOLD

INTERCESSORY PRAYER

How God Can Use Your Prayers to Move Heaven and Earth

Intercessory Prayer Resources
Book • ISBN 978.80307.45166
Student Guide • ISBN 978.08307.45173
DVD • UPC 607135.014621

If God is all-powerful, why does He need us to pray? If we pray and nothing happens, does this mean that God isn't listening? For those who have ever felt that their prayers don't count, *Intercessory Prayer* will show just how vital their prayers are.

Pastor and teacher Dutch Sheets explains the nuts and bolts of prayer, with wisdom, gentleness and humor. This book will inspire readers, give them the courage to pray for the "impossible" and help them find the persistence to see their prayers to completion. It's time to discover our roles as prayer warriors—it can mean the difference between heaven and hell for someone you know!

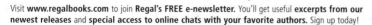

Also from Dutch Sheets

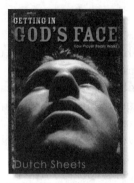

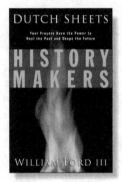

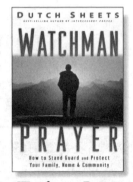

Getting in God's Face
How Prayer Really Works
ISBN 978.08307.38014

History Makers
Your Prayers Have the
Power to Heal the Past
and Shape the Future
ISBN 978.08307.32456
DVD • UPC 607135.008507

Watchman Prayer
How to Stand Guard
and Protect Your Family,
Home and Community
ISBN 978.08307.25687
DVD • UPC 607135.004653

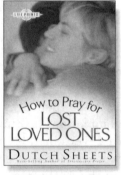

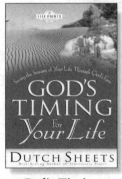

How to Pray for
Lost Loved Ones
How to Pray for the Salvation
of Our Friends and Families
ISBN 978.08307.27650
DVD • UPC 607135.005858

The River of God
Moving in the Flow of
God's Plan for Revival
ISBN 978.08307.20750

God's Timing
for Your Life
Seeing the Season of Your
Life Through God's Eyes
ISBN 978.08307.27636
DVD • UPC 607135.006022